VERTIGO

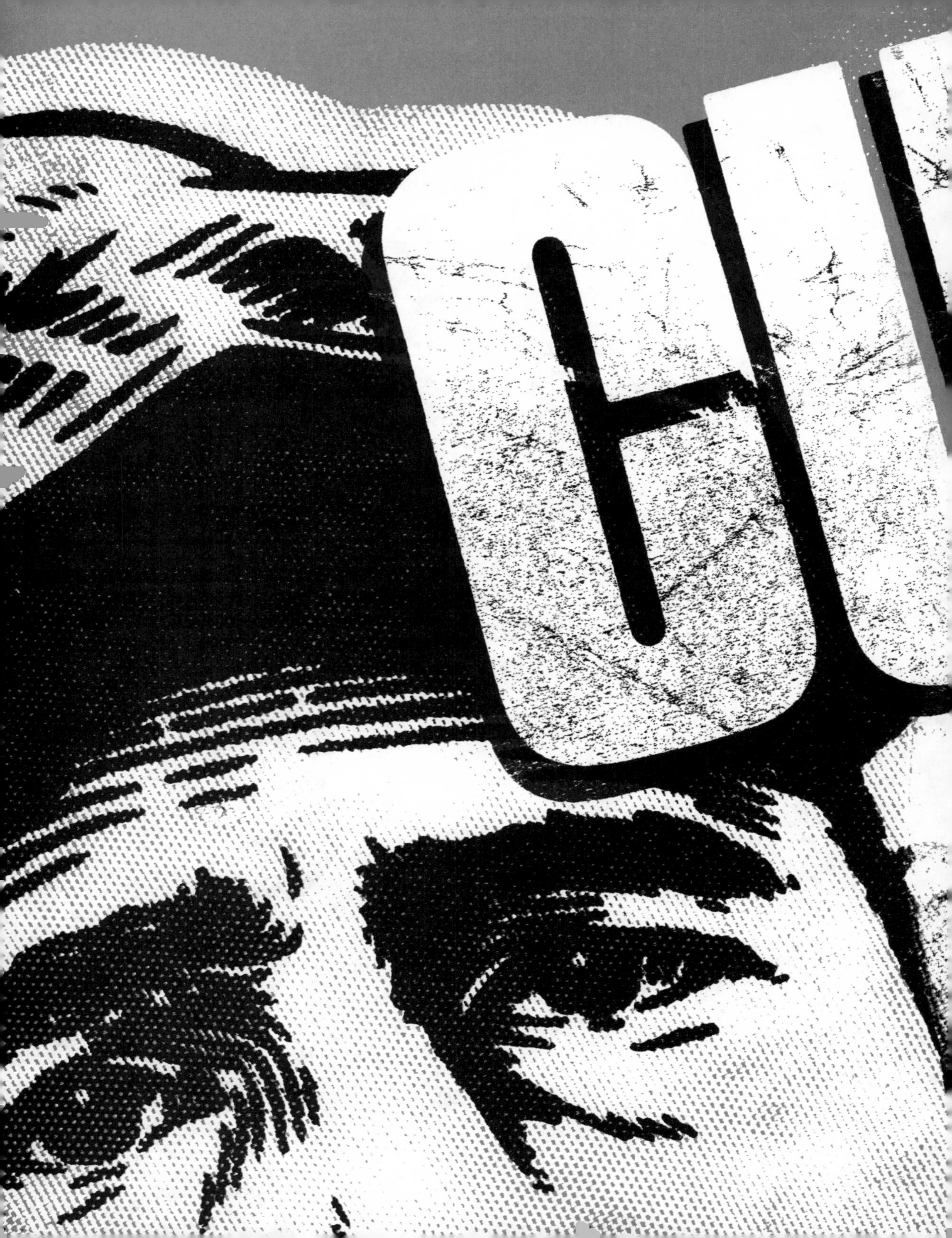

CUBA

my revolution

writer **INVERNA LOCKPEZ**

artist **DEAN HASPIEL**

colorist **JOSÉ VILLARRUBIA** letterer **PAT BROSSEAU**

Author's Note

There were aspects of my life I preferred to forget because they were too painful
to remember. In spite of myself, flashes of past experiences appeared, and in the
process of reconstructing them I learned that testimony is important to the ideals
and endurance of the human spirit, as well as to my own.

This book is for the people of Cuba everywhere who have not been heard, who have
endured economic hardship, who long to express themselves through art without the
fear of imprisonment, and who still fight for the return of freedom once enjoyed.

—Inverna Lockpez

DEDICATIONS

I want to thank Dean Haspiel for encouraging me to tell my story and for an incredibly inspiring and challenging collaboration; my editor, Joan Hilty, for her insightful guidance; Jose Villarrubia for making me love pink again; and my friends who read the manuscript and gave valuable suggestions: Lisa Rainwater, Andy Mele, and Wendy Kesselman. Special thanks to my partner Ali, for working with me on this project with patience and understanding.

—Inverna Lockpez

I'd like to thank my beautiful mother, Barbara Haspiel, for introducing me to Inverna Lockpez, who, over the past two decades, became my second mother and bravely divulged her personal experiences of Cuba. I'm luckier than most human beings to have these two women help shape my life.

I'd like to thank Joan Hilty for being the best editor I've ever worked with. This book could not have happened without her commitment and sensitivity to storytelling and detail. I'd like to give Jose Villarrubia a big bear hug for helping me realize a highly romanticized yet tragic era with the mastery of his colors and painting.

I'd also like to acknowledge the wisdom and support of Michel Fiffe, Jen Ferguson, and DEEP6 Studios.

—Dean Haspiel

Karen Berger SVP - Executive Editor   Joan Hilty Editor   Sarah Litt Assistant Editor
Robbin Brosterman Design Director - Books   Louis Prandi Art Director

DC COMICS
Diane Nelson President, Dan DiDio and Jim Lee Co-Publishers   Geoff Johns Chief Creative Officer
John Rood Executive Vice President, Sales, Marketing and Business Development
Patrick Caldon Executive Vice President, Finance and Administration   Amy Genkins Senior VP-Business and Legal Affairs
Steve Rotterdam Senior VP-Sales and Marketing   John Cunningham VP-Marketing
Terri Cunningham VP-Managing Editor   Alison Gill VP-Manufacturing   David Hyde VP-Publicity
Sue Pohja VP-Book Trade Sales   Alysse Soll VP-Advertising and Custom Publishing
Bob Wayne VP-Sales   Mark Chiarello Art Director

Cover Artist: Dean Haspiel
CUBA: MY REVOLUTION. Published by DC Comics, 1700 Broadway, New York, NY 10019. Copyright © 2010 by Inverna
Lockpez and Dean Haspiel. Artwork on pages 6, 38 and 94 by and © Inverna Lockpez, graphite on paper, Cuba 1960s. All rights
reserved. VERTIGO is a trademark of DC Comics. Printed in the USA. First Printing. DC Comics, a Warner Bros. Entertainment Company.
HC ISBN: 978-1-4012-2217-8   SC ISBN: 978-1-4012-2218-5

SUSTAINABLE
FORESTRY
INITIATIVE
Certified Chain of Custody
Promoting Sustainable
Forest Management

SGS-SFI/COC-US10/81072

PART ONE

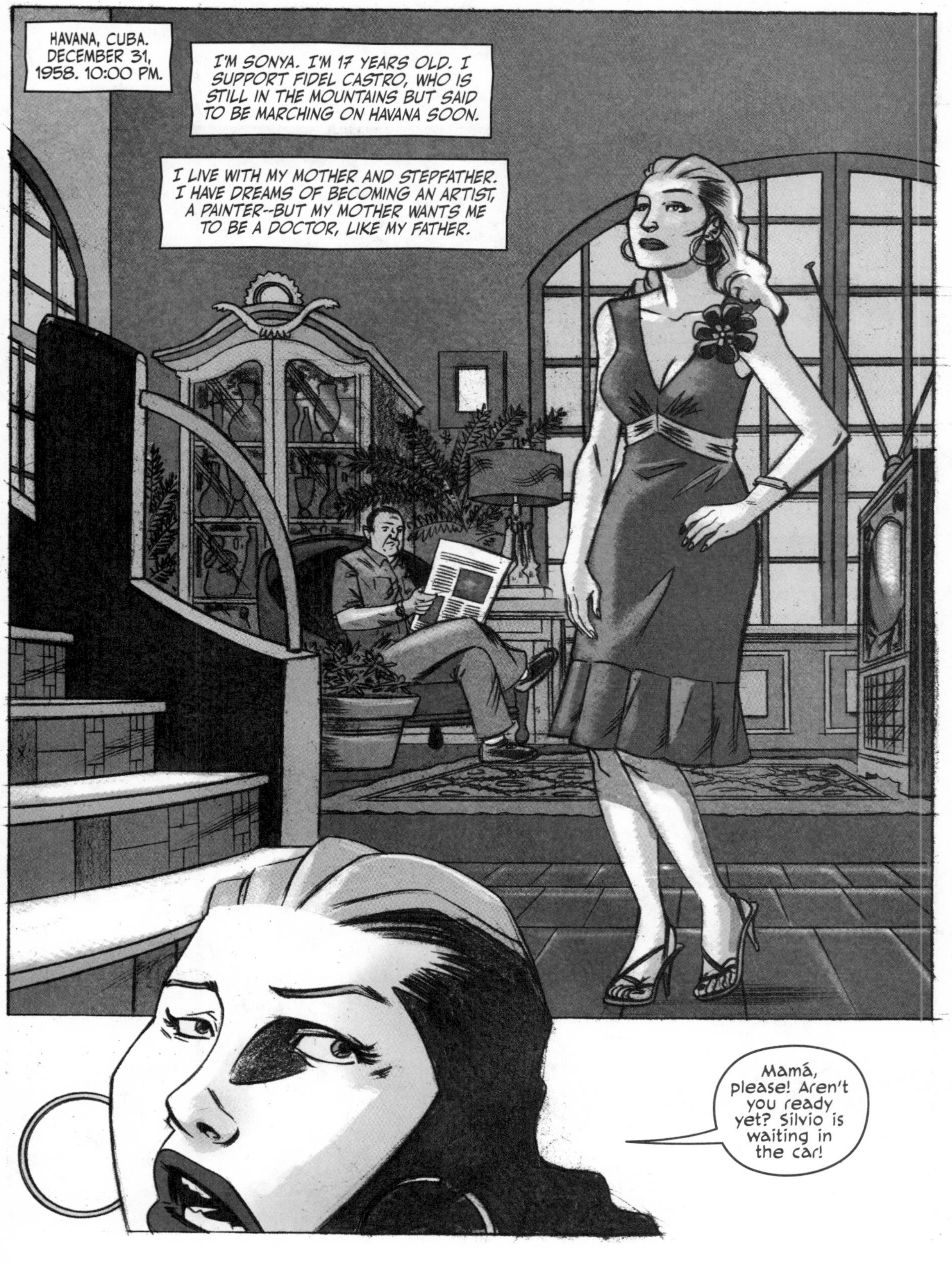
HAVANA, CUBA. DECEMBER 31, 1958. 10:00 PM.
I'M SONYA. I'M 17 YEARS OLD. I SUPPORT FIDEL CASTRO, WHO IS STILL IN THE MOUNTAINS BUT SAID TO BE MARCHING ON HAVANA SOON.
I LIVE WITH MY MOTHER AND STEPFATHER. I HAVE DREAMS OF BECOMING AN ARTIST, A PAINTER--BUT MY MOTHER WANTS ME TO BE A DOCTOR, LIKE MY FATHER.
Mamá, please! Aren't you ready yet? Silvio is waiting in the car!

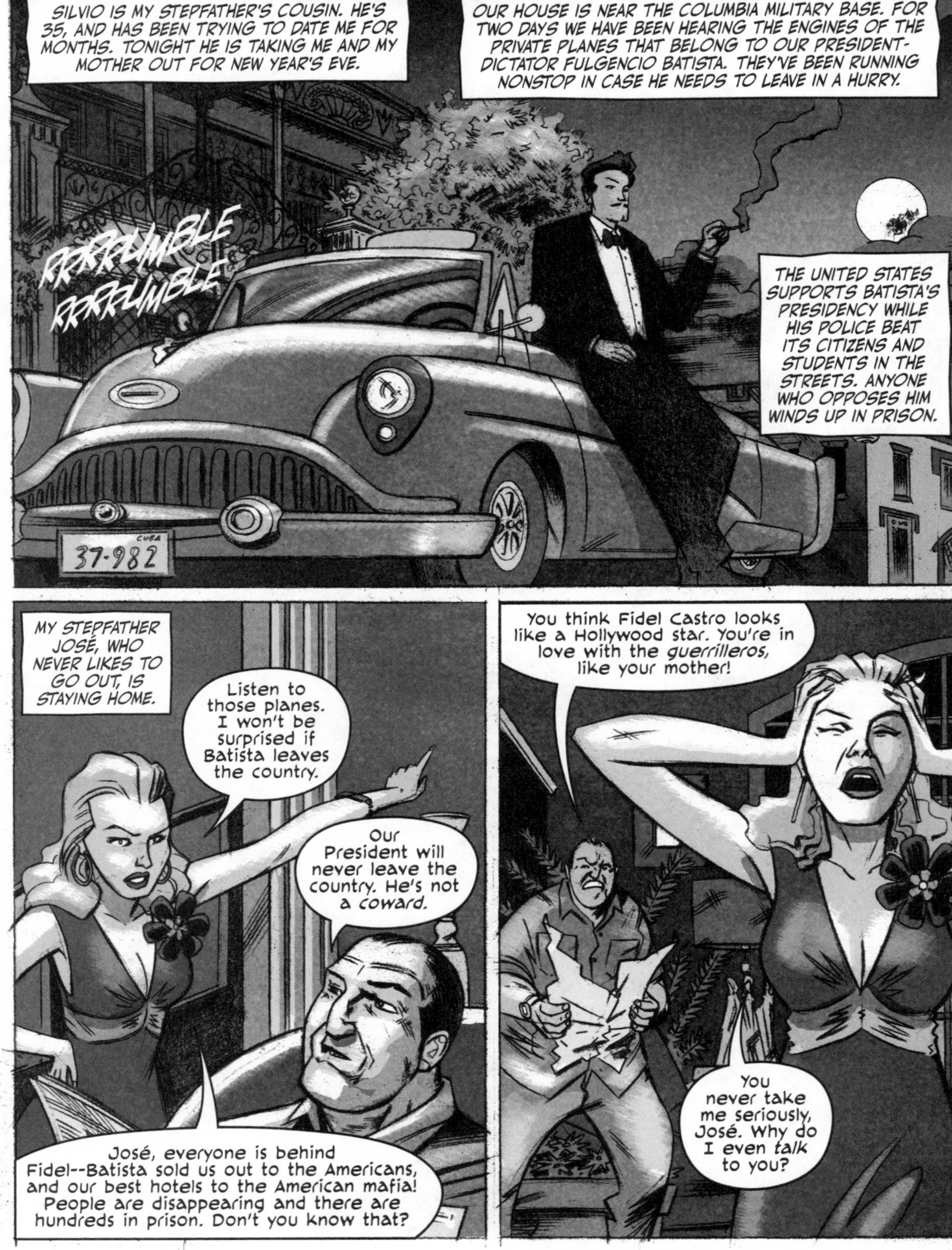
SILVIO IS MY STEPFATHER'S COUSIN. HE'S 35, AND HAS BEEN TRYING TO DATE ME FOR MONTHS. TONIGHT HE IS TAKING ME AND MY MOTHER OUT FOR NEW YEAR'S EVE.
OUR HOUSE IS NEAR THE COLUMBIA MILITARY BASE. FOR TWO DAYS WE HAVE BEEN HEARING THE ENGINES OF THE PRIVATE PLANES THAT BELONG TO OUR PRESIDENT-DICTATOR FULGENCIO BATISTA. THEY'VE BEEN RUNNING NONSTOP IN CASE HE NEEDS TO LEAVE IN A HURRY.
RRRRUMBLE
RRRRUMBLE
THE UNITED STATES SUPPORTS BATISTA'S PRESIDENCY WHILE HIS POLICE BEAT ITS CITIZENS AND STUDENTS IN THE STREETS. ANYONE WHO OPPOSES HIM WINDS UP IN PRISON.
CUBA
37-982
MY STEPFATHER JOSÉ, WHO NEVER LIKES TO GO OUT, IS STAYING HOME.
Listen to those planes. I won't be surprised if Batista leaves the country.
Our President will never leave the country. He's not a *coward.*
José, everyone is behind Fidel--Batista sold us out to the Americans, and our best hotels to the American mafia! People are disappearing and there are hundreds in prison. Don't you know that?
You think Fidel Castro looks like a Hollywood star. You're in love with the *guerrilleros,* like your mother!
You never take me seriously, José. Why do I even *talk* to you?

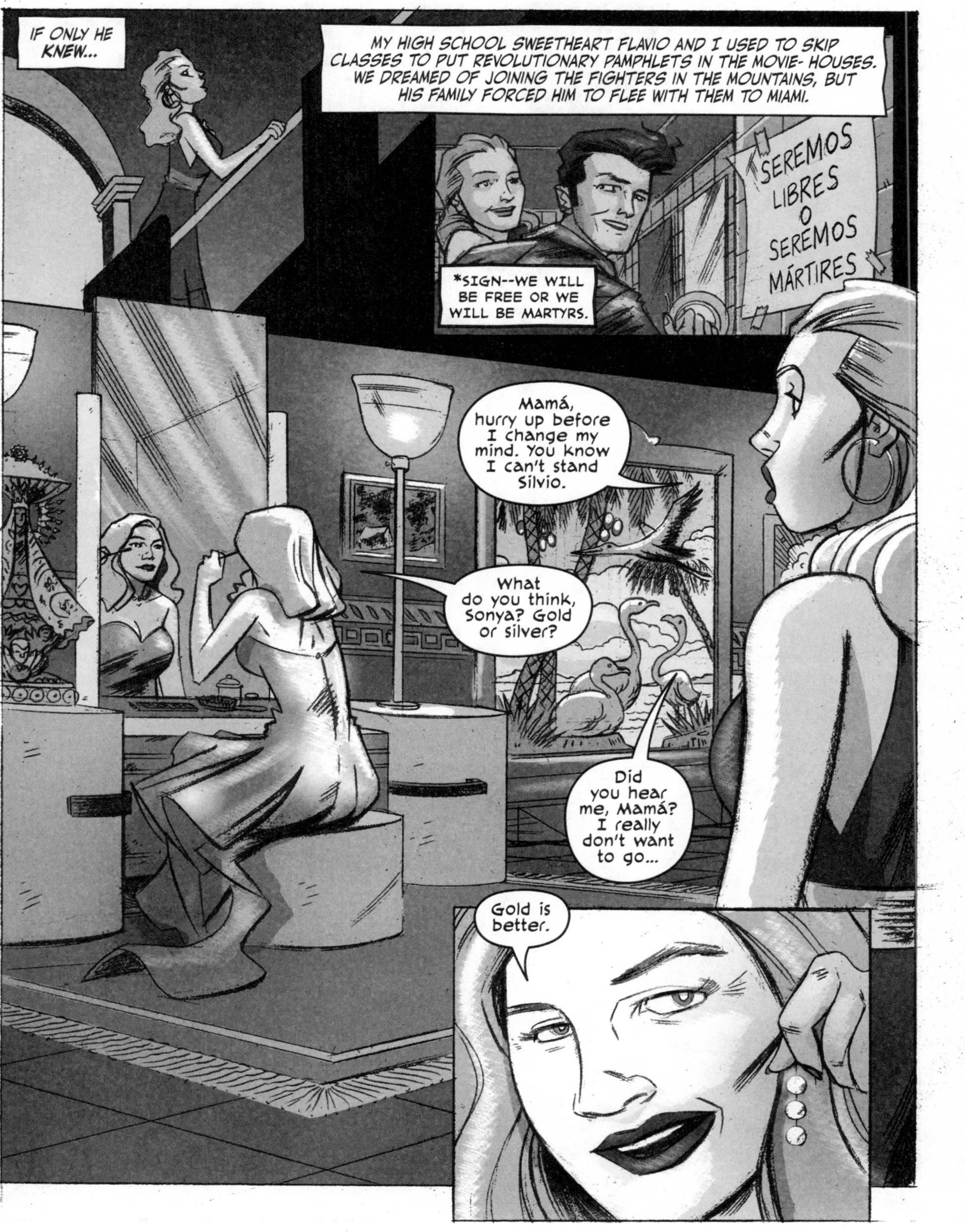
IF ONLY HE KNEW...
MY HIGH SCHOOL SWEETHEART FLAVIO AND I USED TO SKIP CLASSES TO PUT REVOLUTIONARY PAMPHLETS IN THE MOVIE- HOUSES. WE DREAMED OF JOINING THE FIGHTERS IN THE MOUNTAINS, BUT HIS FAMILY FORCED HIM TO FLEE WITH THEM TO MIAMI.
SEREMOS LIBRES O SEREMOS MÁRTIRES
*SIGN--WE WILL BE FREE OR WE WILL BE MARTYRS.
Mamá, hurry up before I change my mind. You know I can't stand Silvio.
What do you think, Sonya? Gold or silver?
Did you hear me, Mamá? I really don't want to go...
Gold is better.

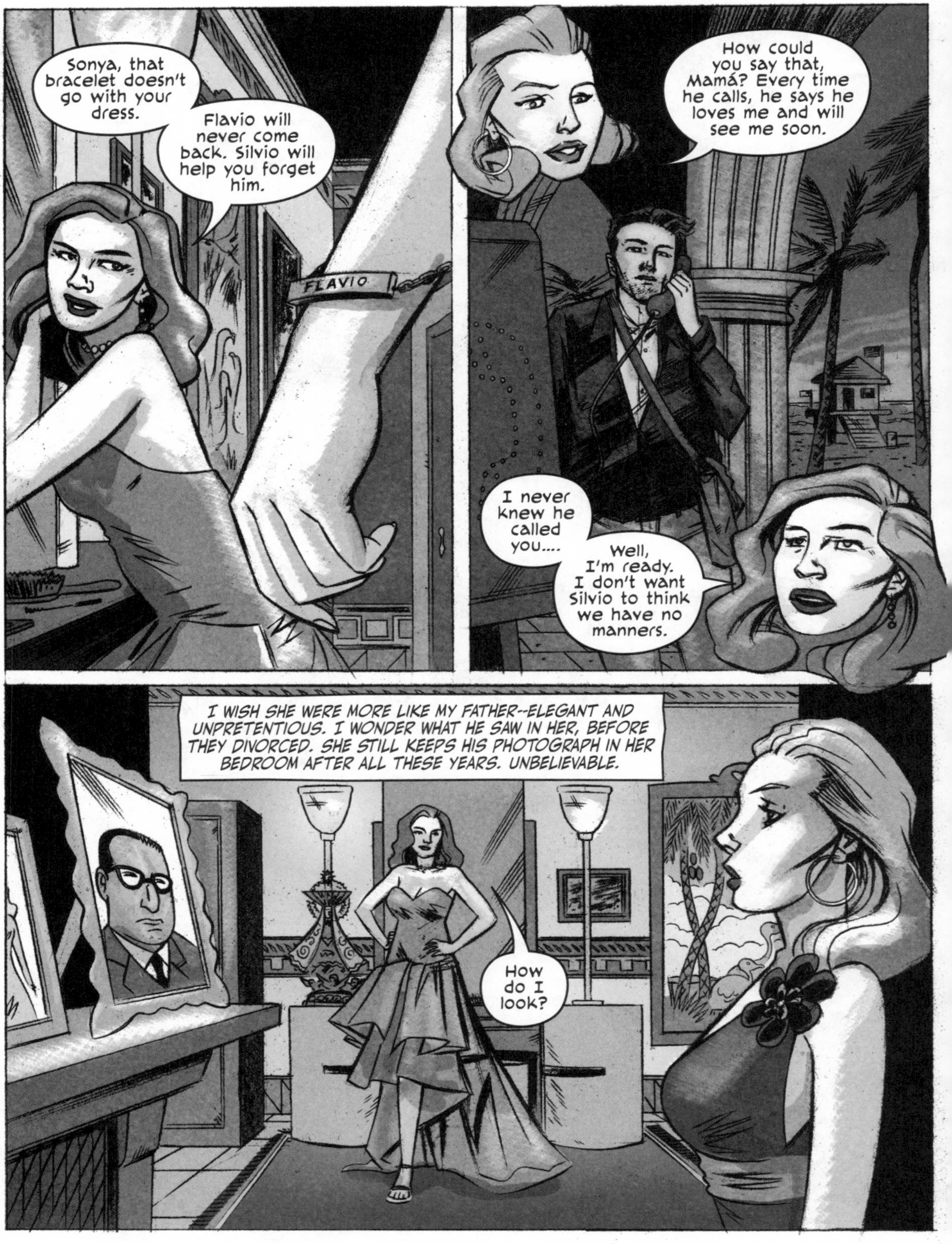
Sonya, that bracelet doesn't go with your dress.
Flavio will never come back. Silvio will help you forget him.
FLAVIO
How could you say that, Mamá? Every time he calls, he says he loves me and will see me soon.
I never knew he called you....
Well, I'm ready. I don't want Silvio to think we have no manners.
I WISH SHE WERE MORE LIKE MY FATHER--ELEGANT AND UNPRETENTIOUS. I WONDER WHAT HE SAW IN HER, BEFORE THEY DIVORCED. SHE STILL KEEPS HIS PHOTOGRAPH IN HER BEDROOM AFTER ALL THESE YEARS. UNBELIEVABLE.
How do I look?

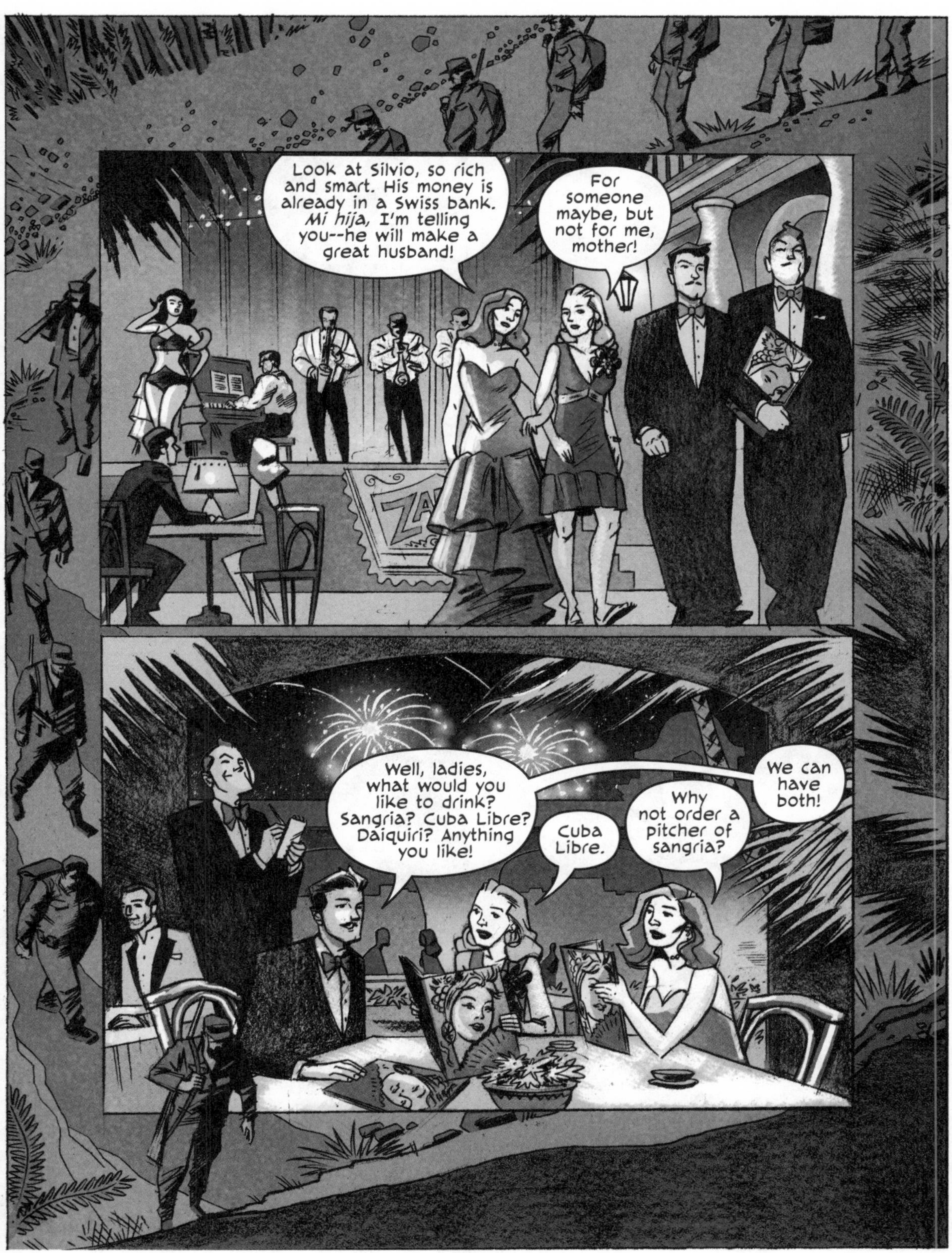
Look at Silvio, so rich and smart. His money is already in a Swiss bank. *Mi hija,* I'm telling you--he will make a great husband!
For someone maybe, but not for me, mother!
Well, ladies, what would you like to drink? Sangria? Cuba Libre? Daiquiri? Anything you like!
Cuba Libre.
Why not order a pitcher of sangria?
We can have both!

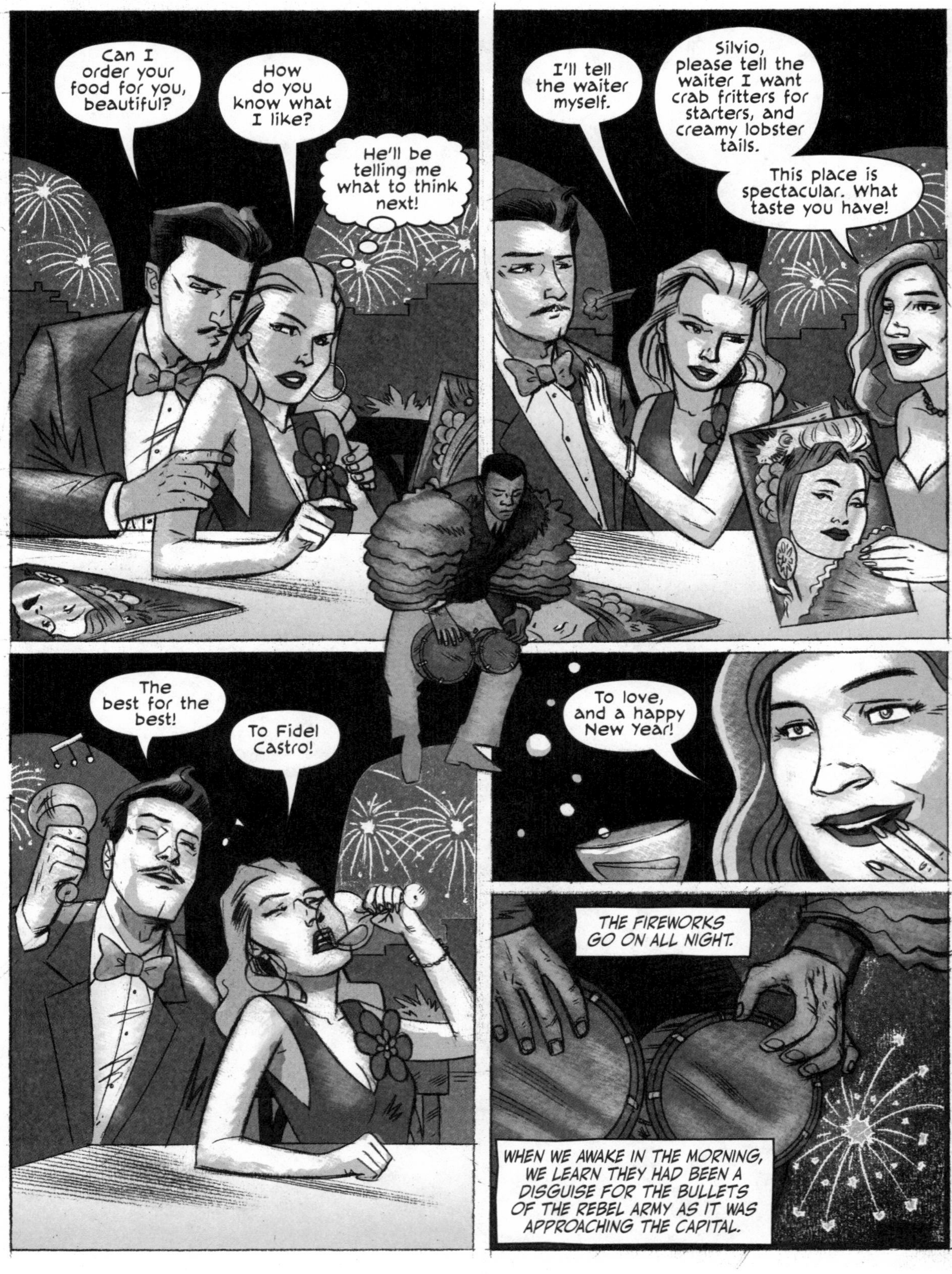
Can I order your food for you, beautiful?
How do you know what I like?
He'll be telling me what to think next!
I'll tell the waiter myself.
Silvio, please tell the waiter I want crab fritters for starters, and creamy lobster tails.
This place is spectacular. What taste you have!
The best for the best!
To Fidel Castro!
To love, and a happy New Year!
THE FIREWORKS GO ON ALL NIGHT.
WHEN WE AWAKE IN THE MORNING, WE LEARN THEY HAD BEEN A DISGUISE FOR THE BULLETS OF THE REBEL ARMY AS IT WAS APPROACHING THE CAPITAL.

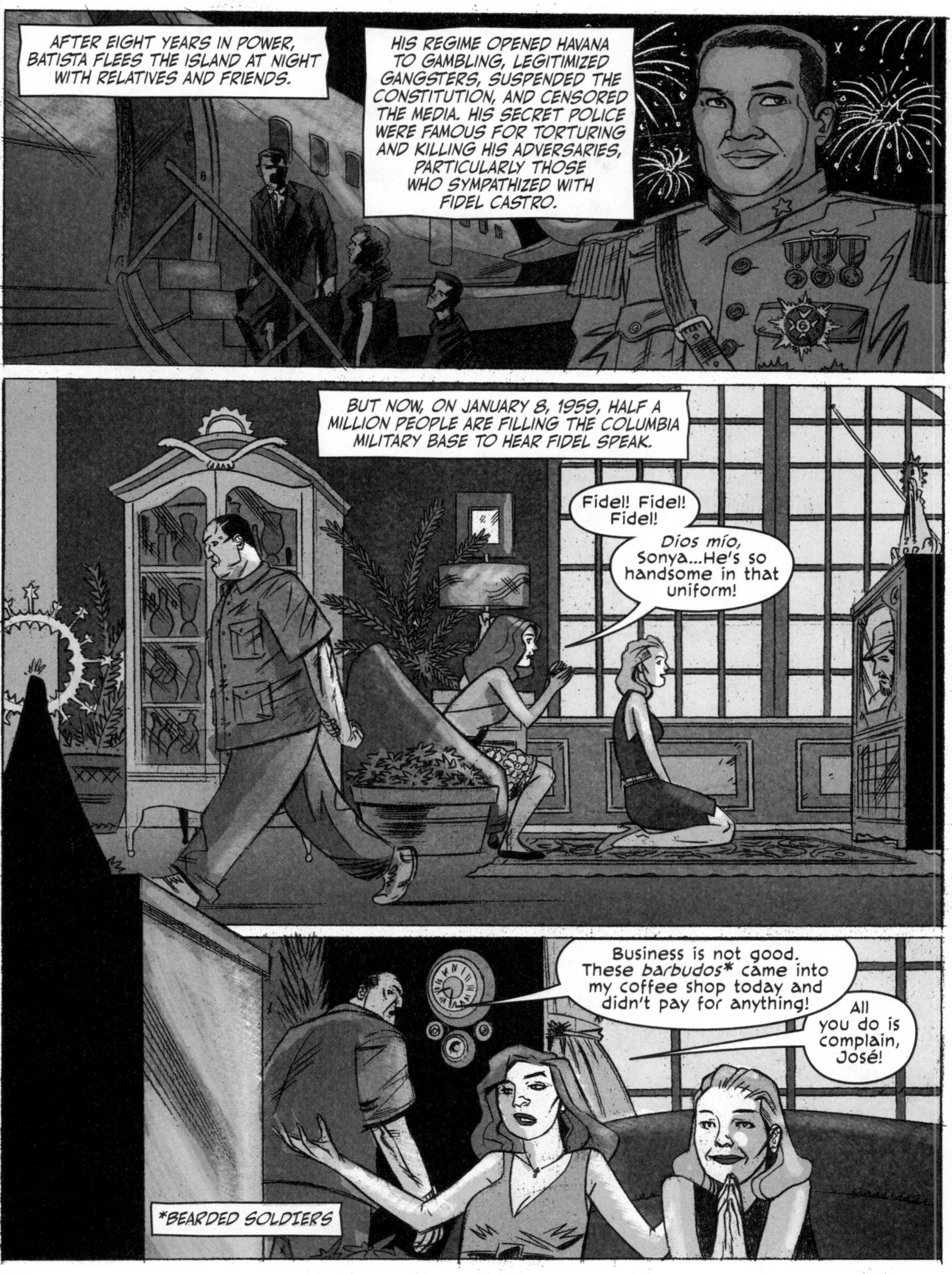
AFTER EIGHT YEARS IN POWER, BATISTA FLEES THE ISLAND AT NIGHT WITH RELATIVES AND FRIENDS.
HIS REGIME OPENED HAVANA TO GAMBLING, LEGITIMIZED GANGSTERS, SUSPENDED THE CONSTITUTION, AND CENSORED THE MEDIA. HIS SECRET POLICE WERE FAMOUS FOR TORTURING AND KILLING HIS ADVERSARIES, PARTICULARLY THOSE WHO SYMPATHIZED WITH FIDEL CASTRO.
BUT NOW, ON JANUARY 8, 1959, HALF A MILLION PEOPLE ARE FILLING THE COLUMBIA MILITARY BASE TO HEAR FIDEL SPEAK.
Fidel! Fidel! Fidel!
Dios mío, Sonya...He's so handsome in that uniform!
Business is not good. These *barbudos** came into my coffee shop today and didn't pay for anything!
All you do is complain, José!
*BEARDED SOLDIERS

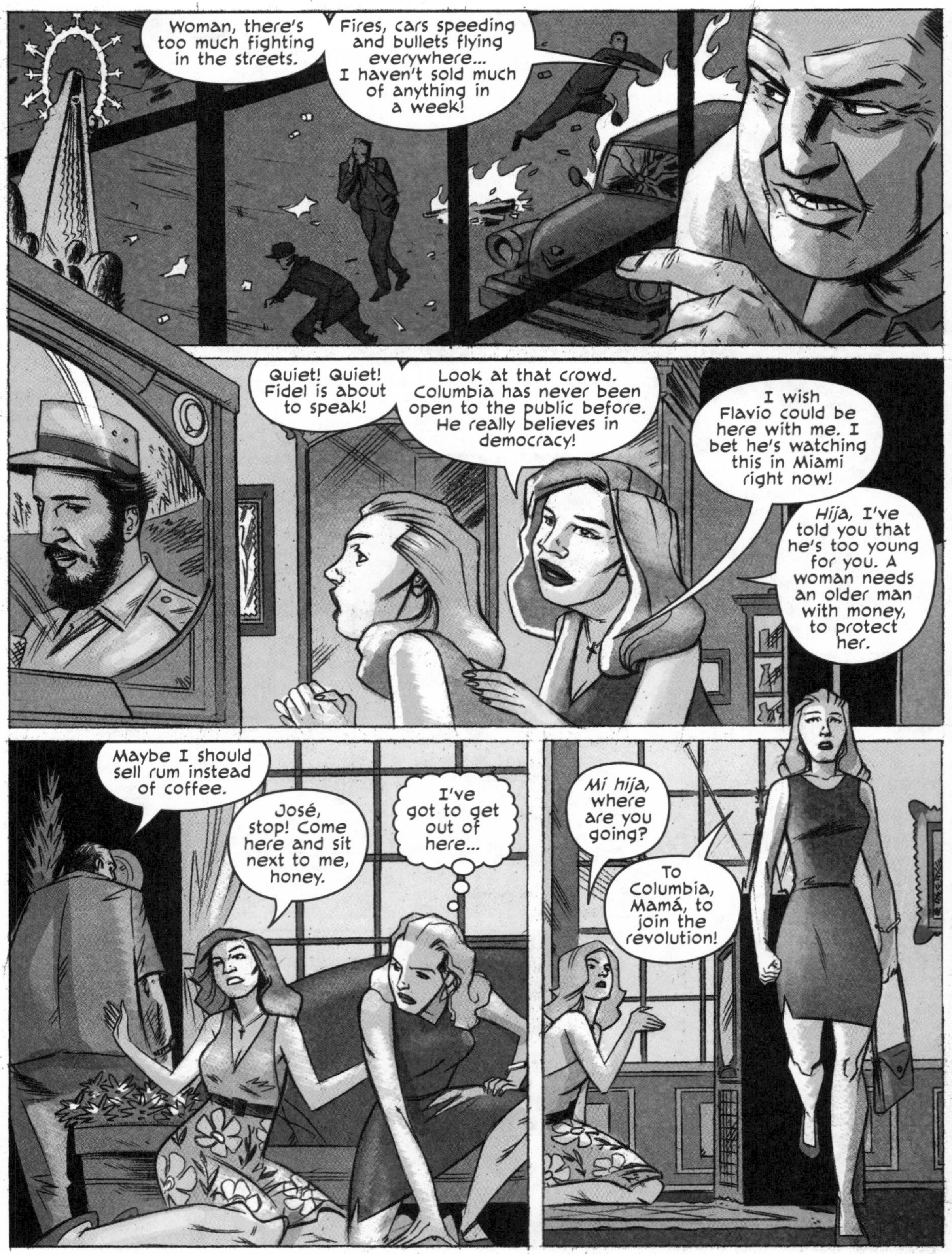
Woman, there's too much fighting in the streets.
Fires, cars speeding and bullets flying everywhere... I haven't sold much of anything in a week!
Quiet! Quiet! Fidel is about to speak!
Look at that crowd. Columbia has never been open to the public before. He really believes in democracy!
I wish Flavio could be here with me. I bet he's watching this in Miami right now!
Hija, I've told you that he's too young for you. A woman needs an older man with money, to protect her.
Maybe I should sell rum instead of coffee.
José, stop! Come here and sit next to me, honey.
I've got to get out of here...
Mi hija, where are you going?
To Columbia, Mamá, to join the revolution!

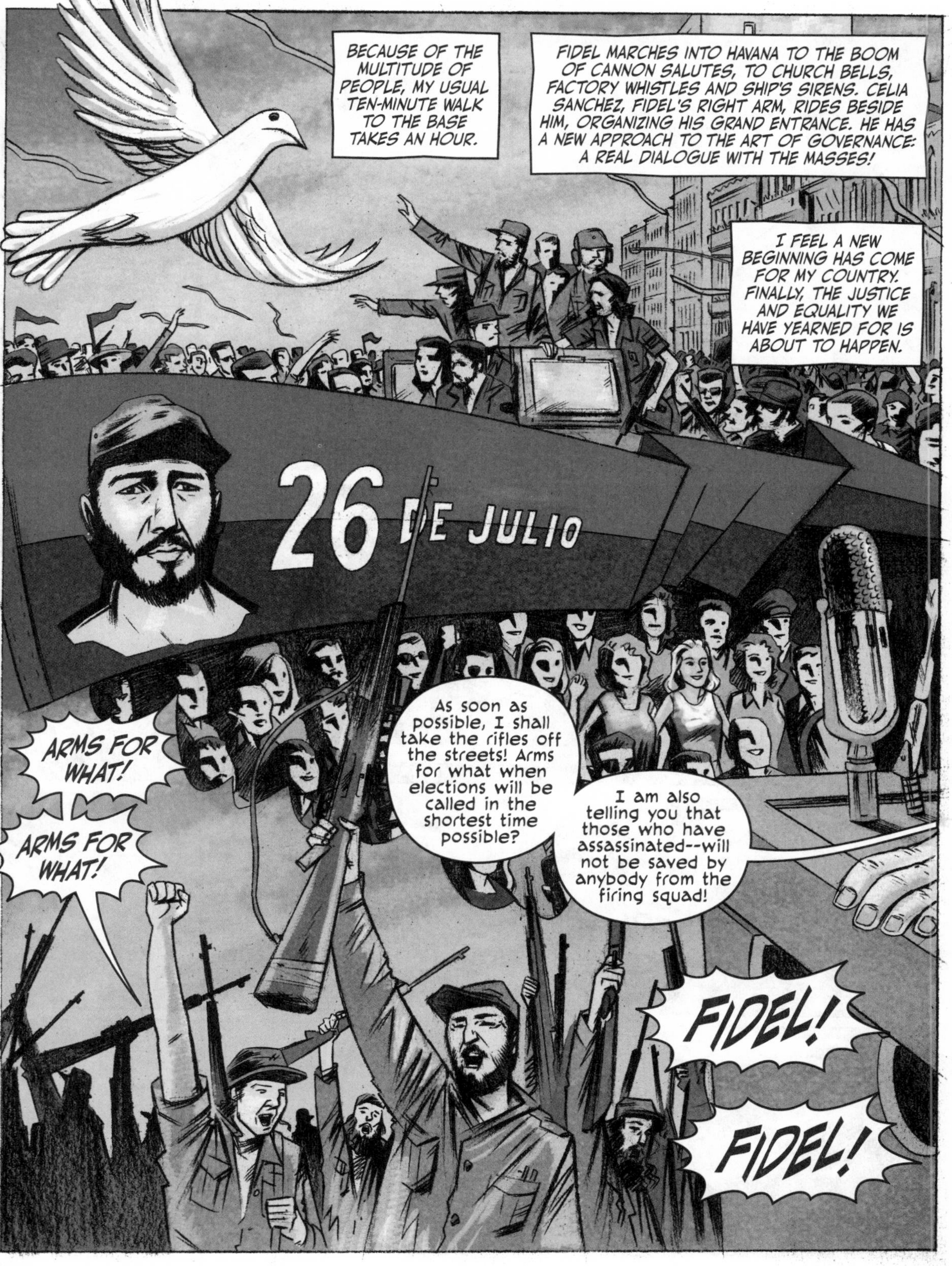
BECAUSE OF THE MULTITUDE OF PEOPLE, MY USUAL TEN-MINUTE WALK TO THE BASE TAKES AN HOUR.
FIDEL MARCHES INTO HAVANA TO THE BOOM OF CANNON SALUTES, TO CHURCH BELLS, FACTORY WHISTLES AND SHIP'S SIRENS. CELIA SANCHEZ, FIDEL'S RIGHT ARM, RIDES BESIDE HIM, ORGANIZING HIS GRAND ENTRANCE. HE HAS A NEW APPROACH TO THE ART OF GOVERNANCE: A REAL DIALOGUE WITH THE MASSES!
I FEEL A NEW BEGINNING HAS COME FOR MY COUNTRY. FINALLY, THE JUSTICE AND EQUALITY WE HAVE YEARNED FOR IS ABOUT TO HAPPEN.
26 DE JULIO
As soon as possible, I shall take the rifles off the streets! Arms for what when elections will be called in the shortest time possible?
I am also telling you that those who have assassinated--will not be saved by anybody from the firing squad!
ARMS FOR WHAT!
ARMS FOR WHAT!
FIDEL!
FIDEL!

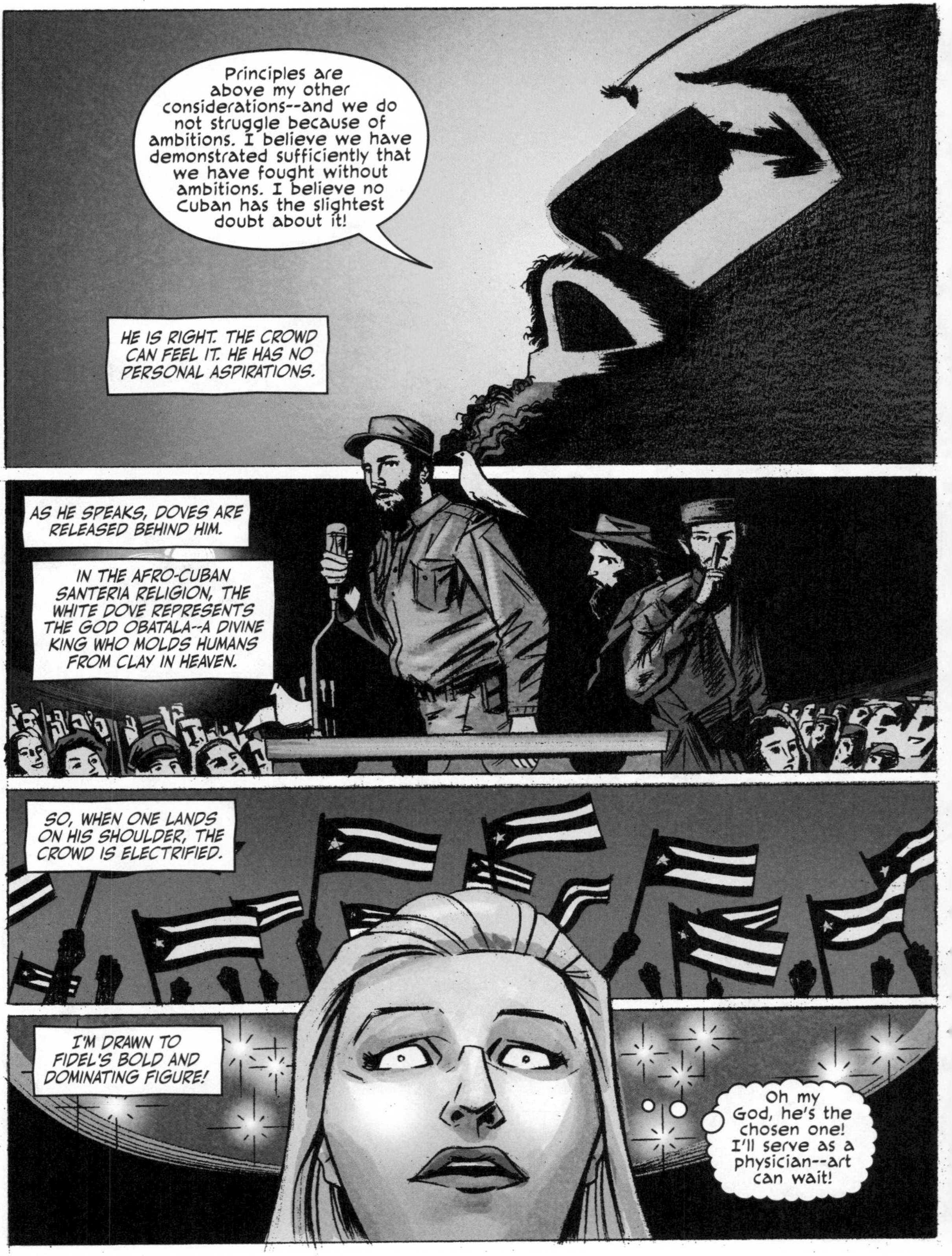
Principles are above my other considerations--and we do not struggle because of ambitions. I believe we have demonstrated sufficiently that we have fought without ambitions. I believe no Cuban has the slightest doubt about it!
HE IS RIGHT. THE CROWD CAN FEEL IT. HE HAS NO PERSONAL ASPIRATIONS.
AS HE SPEAKS, DOVES ARE RELEASED BEHIND HIM.
IN THE AFRO-CUBAN SANTERIA RELIGION, THE WHITE DOVE REPRESENTS THE GOD OBATALA--A DIVINE KING WHO MOLDS HUMANS FROM CLAY IN HEAVEN.
SO, WHEN ONE LANDS ON HIS SHOULDER, THE CROWD IS ELECTRIFIED.
I'M DRAWN TO FIDEL'S BOLD AND DOMINATING FIGURE!
Oh my God, he's the chosen one! I'll serve as a physician--art can wait!

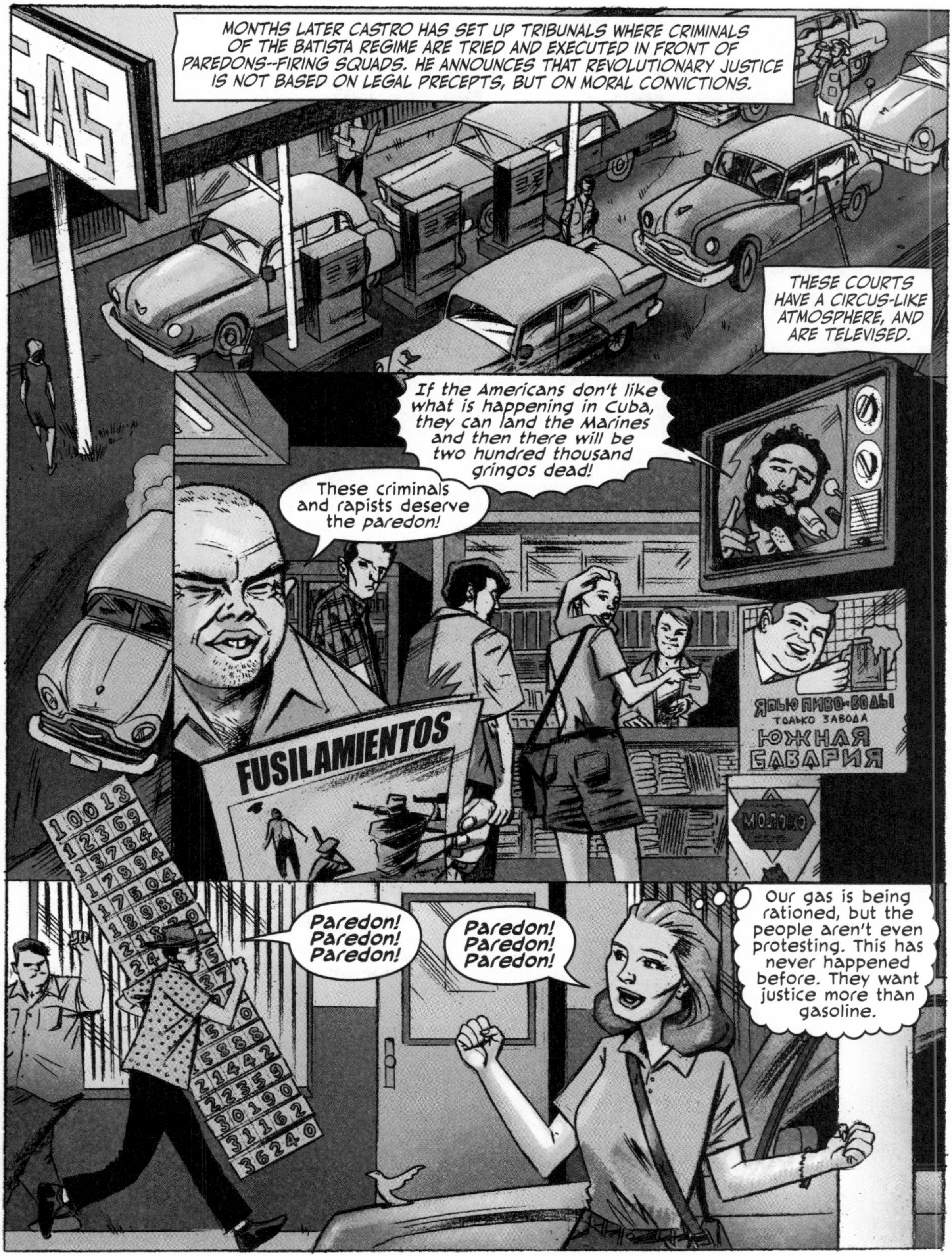
MONTHS LATER CASTRO HAS SET UP TRIBUNALS WHERE CRIMINALS OF THE BATISTA REGIME ARE TRIED AND EXECUTED IN FRONT OF PAREDONS--FIRING SQUADS. HE ANNOUNCES THAT REVOLUTIONARY JUSTICE IS NOT BASED ON LEGAL PRECEPTS, BUT ON MORAL CONVICTIONS.
GAS
THESE COURTS HAVE A CIRCUS-LIKE ATMOSPHERE, AND ARE TELEVISED.
If the Americans don't like what is happening in Cuba, they can land the Marines and then there will be two hundred thousand gringos dead!
These criminals and rapists deserve the *paredon!*
FUSILAMIENTOS
ЯПЬЮ ПИВО-ВОДЫ!
ТОЛЬКО ЗАВОДА
ЮЖНАЯ БАВАРИЯ
МОЛОКО
Paredon! Paredon! Paredon!
Paredon! Paredon! Paredon!
Our gas is being rationed, but the people aren't even protesting. This has never happened before. They want justice more than gasoline.

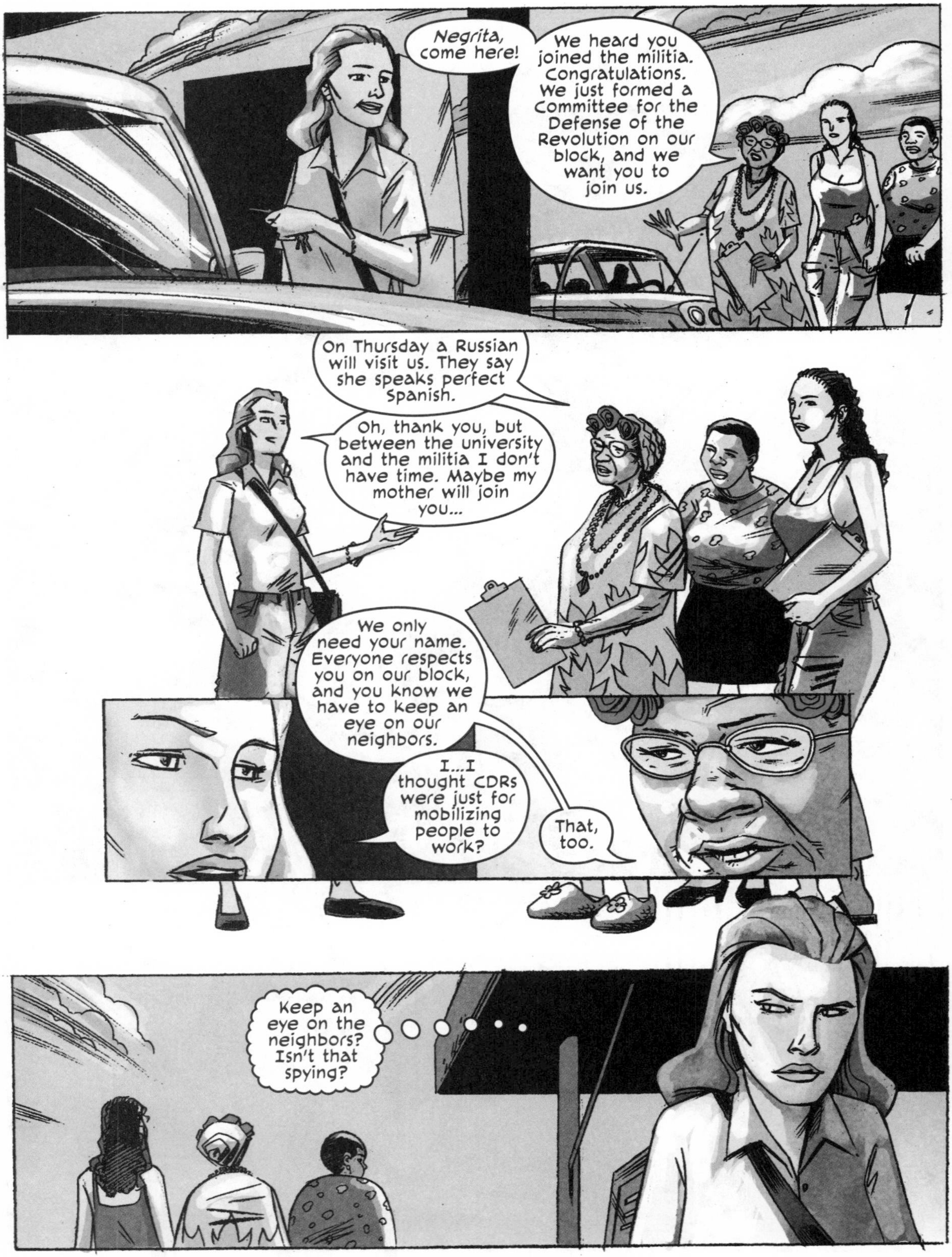

Negrita, come here!
We heard you joined the militia. Congratulations. We just formed a Committee for the Defense of the Revolution on our block, and we want you to join us.
On Thursday a Russian will visit us. They say she speaks perfect Spanish.
Oh, thank you, but between the university and the militia I don't have time. Maybe my mother will join you...
We only need your name. Everyone respects you on our block, and you know we have to keep an eye on our neighbors.
I...I thought CDRs were just for mobilizing people to work?
That, too.
Keep an eye on the neighbors? Isn't that spying?

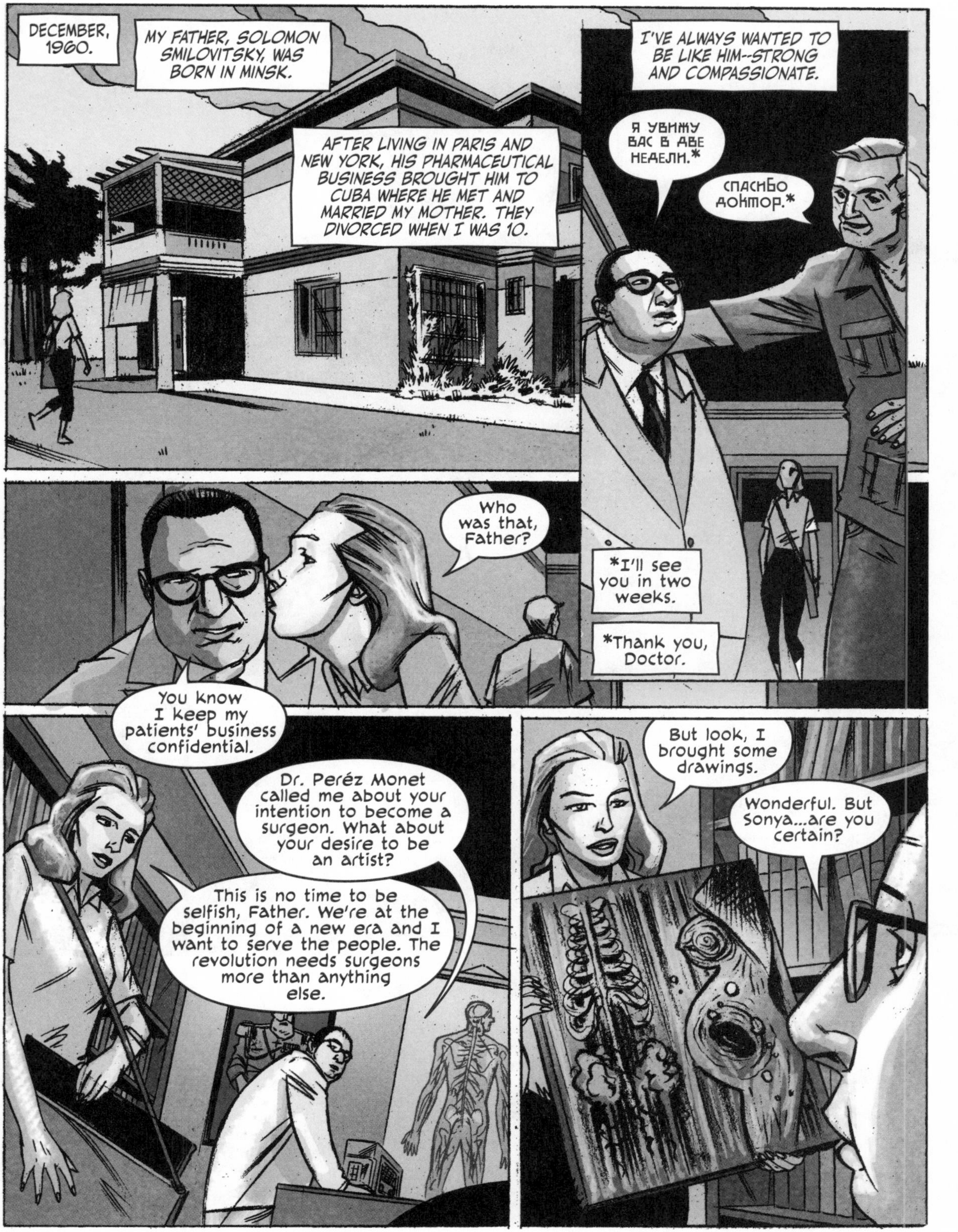
DECEMBER, 1960.
MY FATHER, SOLOMON SMILOVITSKY, WAS BORN IN MINSK.
AFTER LIVING IN PARIS AND NEW YORK, HIS PHARMACEUTICAL BUSINESS BROUGHT HIM TO CUBA WHERE HE MET AND MARRIED MY MOTHER. THEY DIVORCED WHEN I WAS 10.
I'VE ALWAYS WANTED TO BE LIKE HIM--STRONG AND COMPASSIONATE.
Я УВИЖУ ВАС В ДВЕ НЕДЕЛИ.*
СПАСИБО ДОКТОР.*
*I'll see you in two weeks.
*Thank you, Doctor.
Who was that, Father?
You know I keep my patients' business confidential.
Dr. Peréz Monet called me about your intention to become a surgeon. What about your desire to be an artist?
This is no time to be selfish, Father. We're at the beginning of a new era and I want to serve the people. The revolution needs surgeons more than anything else.
But look, I brought some drawings.
Wonderful. But Sonya...are you certain?

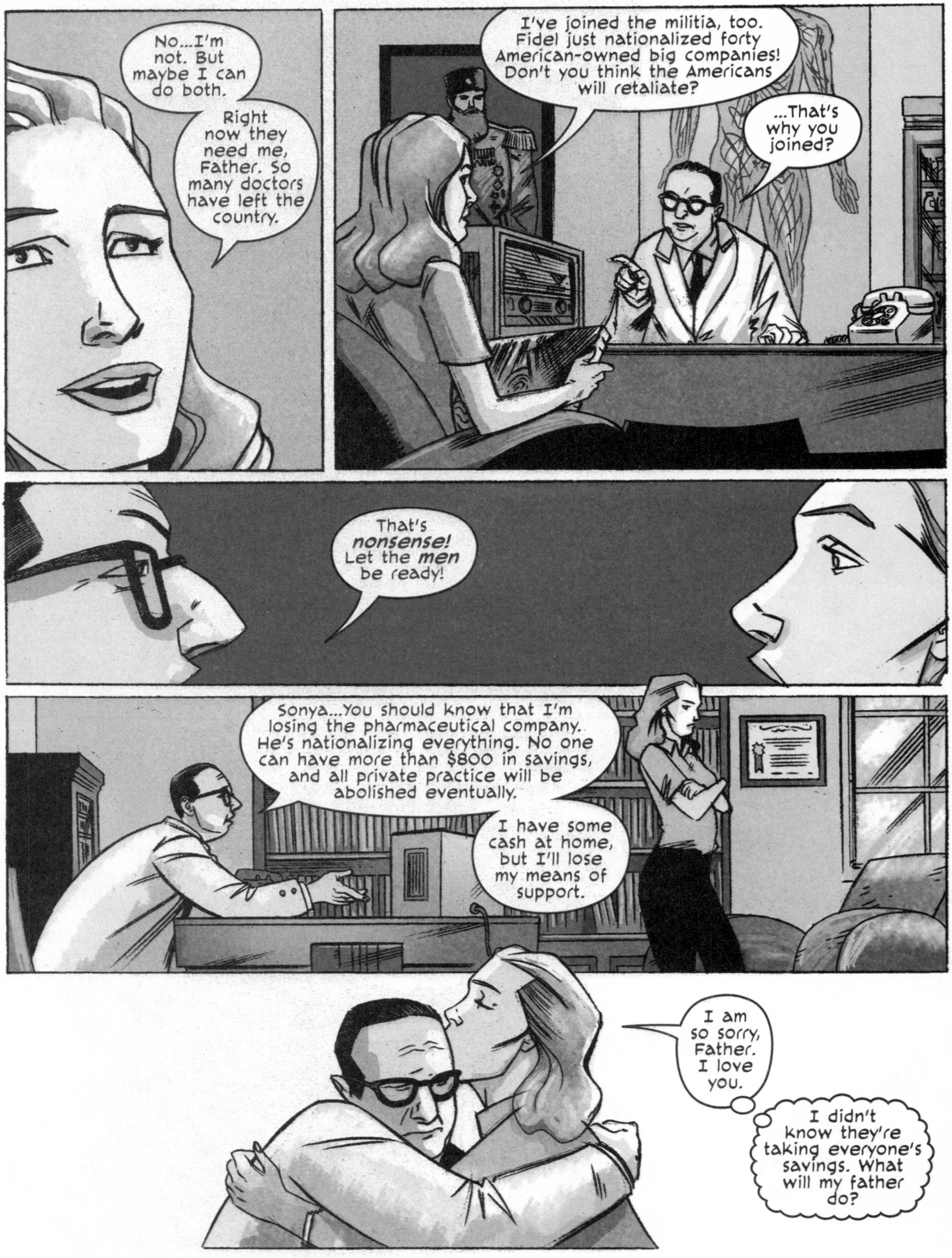
No...I'm not. But maybe I can do both.
Right now they need me, Father. So many doctors have left the country.
I've joined the militia, too. Fidel just nationalized forty American-owned big companies! Don't you think the Americans will retaliate?
...That's why you joined?
That's *nonsense!* Let the *men* be ready!
Sonya...You should know that I'm losing the pharmaceutical company. He's nationalizing everything. No one can have more than $800 in savings, and all private practice will be abolished eventually.
I have some cash at home, but I'll lose my means of support.
I am so sorry, Father. I love you.
I didn't know they're taking everyone's savings. What will my father do?

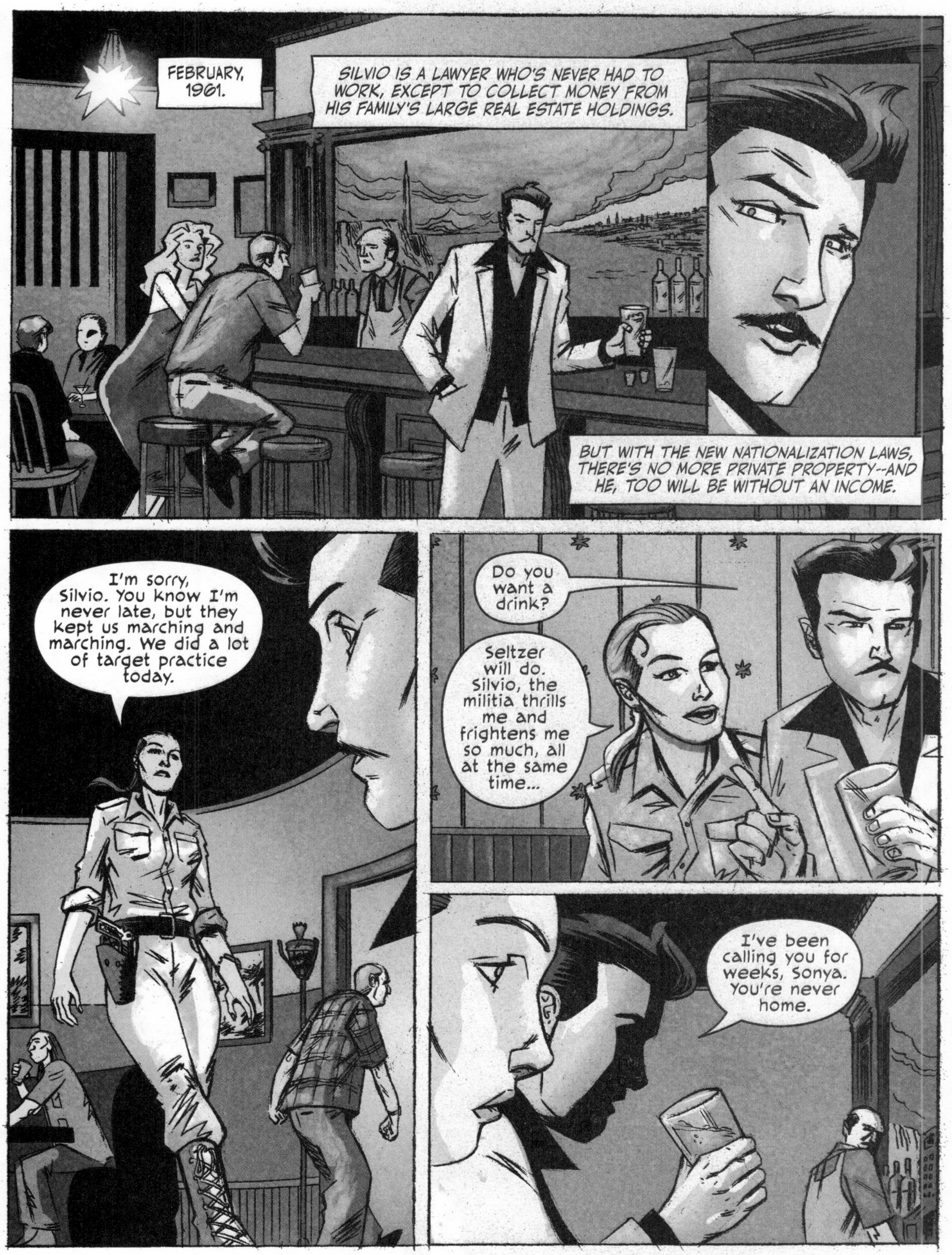

FEBRUARY, 1961.
SILVIO IS A LAWYER WHO'S NEVER HAD TO WORK, EXCEPT TO COLLECT MONEY FROM HIS FAMILY'S LARGE REAL ESTATE HOLDINGS.
BUT WITH THE NEW NATIONALIZATION LAWS, THERE'S NO MORE PRIVATE PROPERTY--AND HE, TOO WILL BE WITHOUT AN INCOME.
I'm sorry, Silvio. You know I'm never late, but they kept us marching and marching. We did a lot of target practice today.
Do you want a drink?
Seltzer will do. Silvio, the militia thrills me and frightens me so much, all at the same time...
I've been calling you for weeks, Sonya. You're never home.

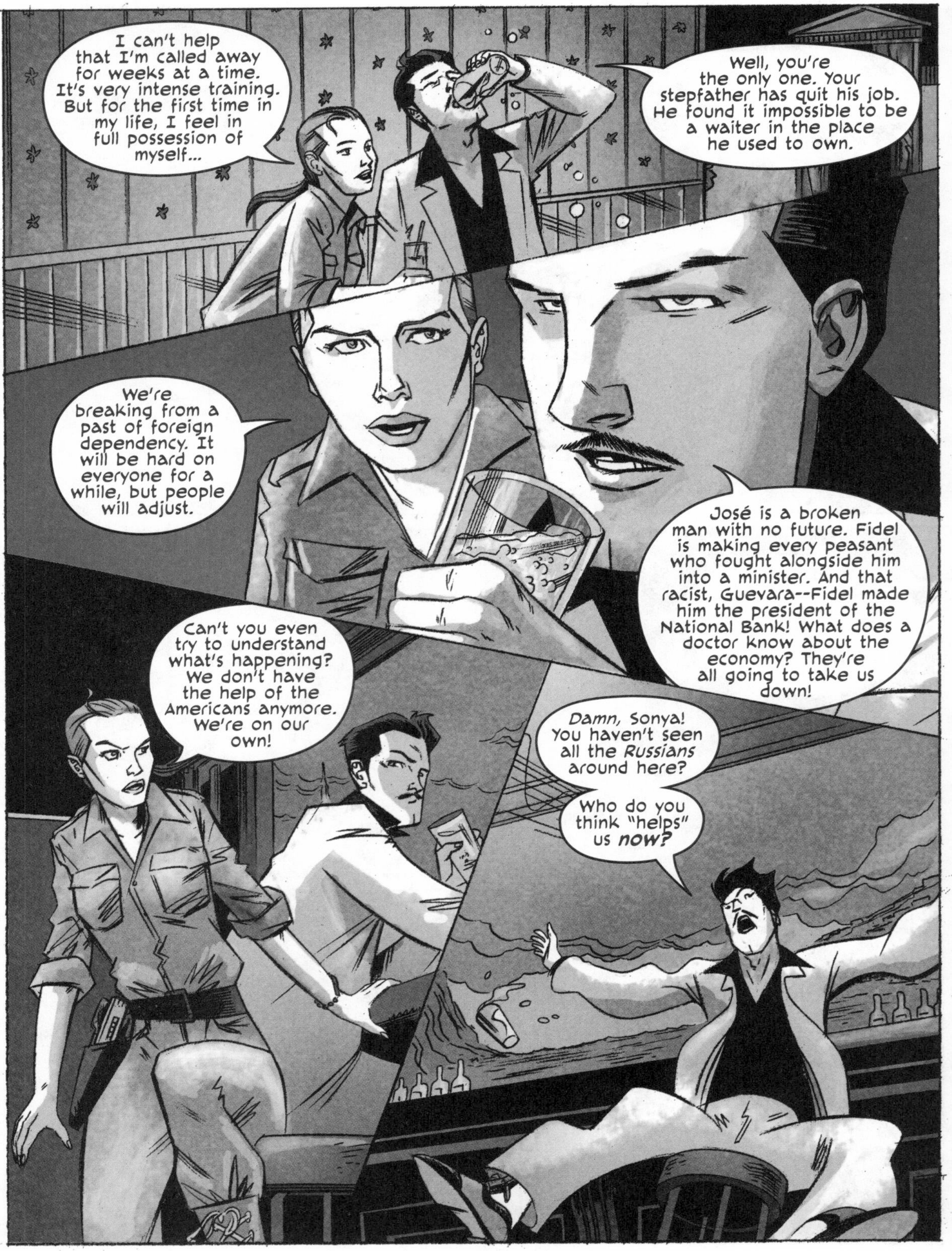
I can't help that I'm called away for weeks at a time. It's very intense training. But for the first time in my life, I feel in full possession of myself...
Well, you're the only one. Your stepfather has quit his job. He found it impossible to be a waiter in the place he used to own.
We're breaking from a past of foreign dependency. It will be hard on everyone for a while, but people will adjust.
José is a broken man with no future. Fidel is making every peasant who fought alongside him into a minister. And that racist, Guevara--Fidel made him the president of the National Bank! What does a doctor know about the economy? They're all going to take us down!
Can't you even try to understand what's happening? We don't have the help of the Americans anymore. We're on our own!
Damn, Sonya! You haven't seen all the *Russians* around here?
Who do you think "helps" us ***now?***

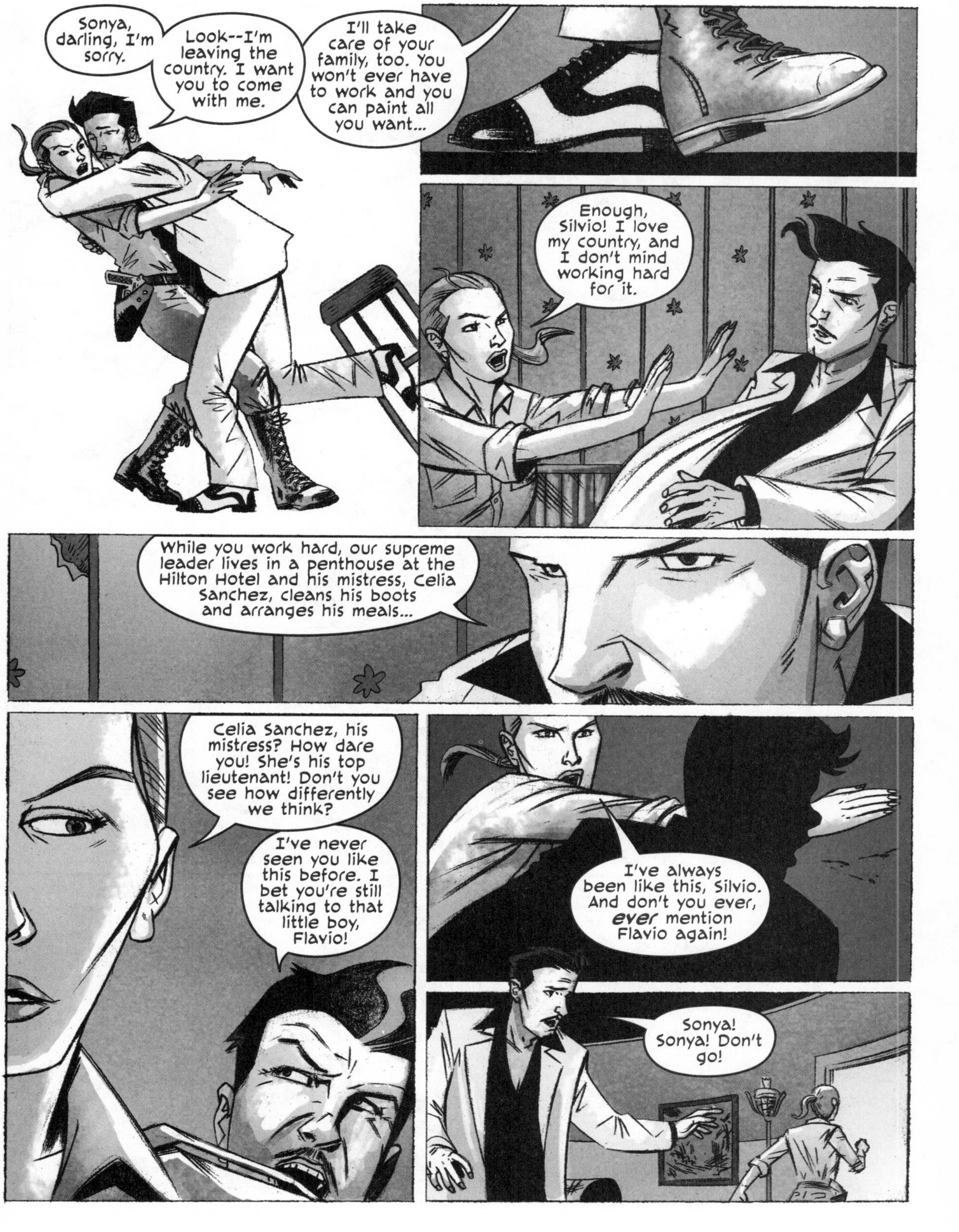

Sonya, darling, I'm sorry.
Look--I'm leaving the country. I want you to come with me.
I'll take care of your family, too. You won't ever have to work and you can paint all you want...
Enough, Silvio! I love my country, and I don't mind working hard for it.
While you work hard, our supreme leader lives in a penthouse at the Hilton Hotel and his mistress, Celia Sanchez, cleans his boots and arranges his meals...
Celia Sanchez, his mistress? How dare you! She's his top lieutenant! Don't you see how differently we think?
I've never seen you like this before. I bet you're still talking to that little boy, Flavio!
I've always been like this, Silvio. And don't you ever, *ever* mention Flavio again!
Sonya! Sonya! Don't go!

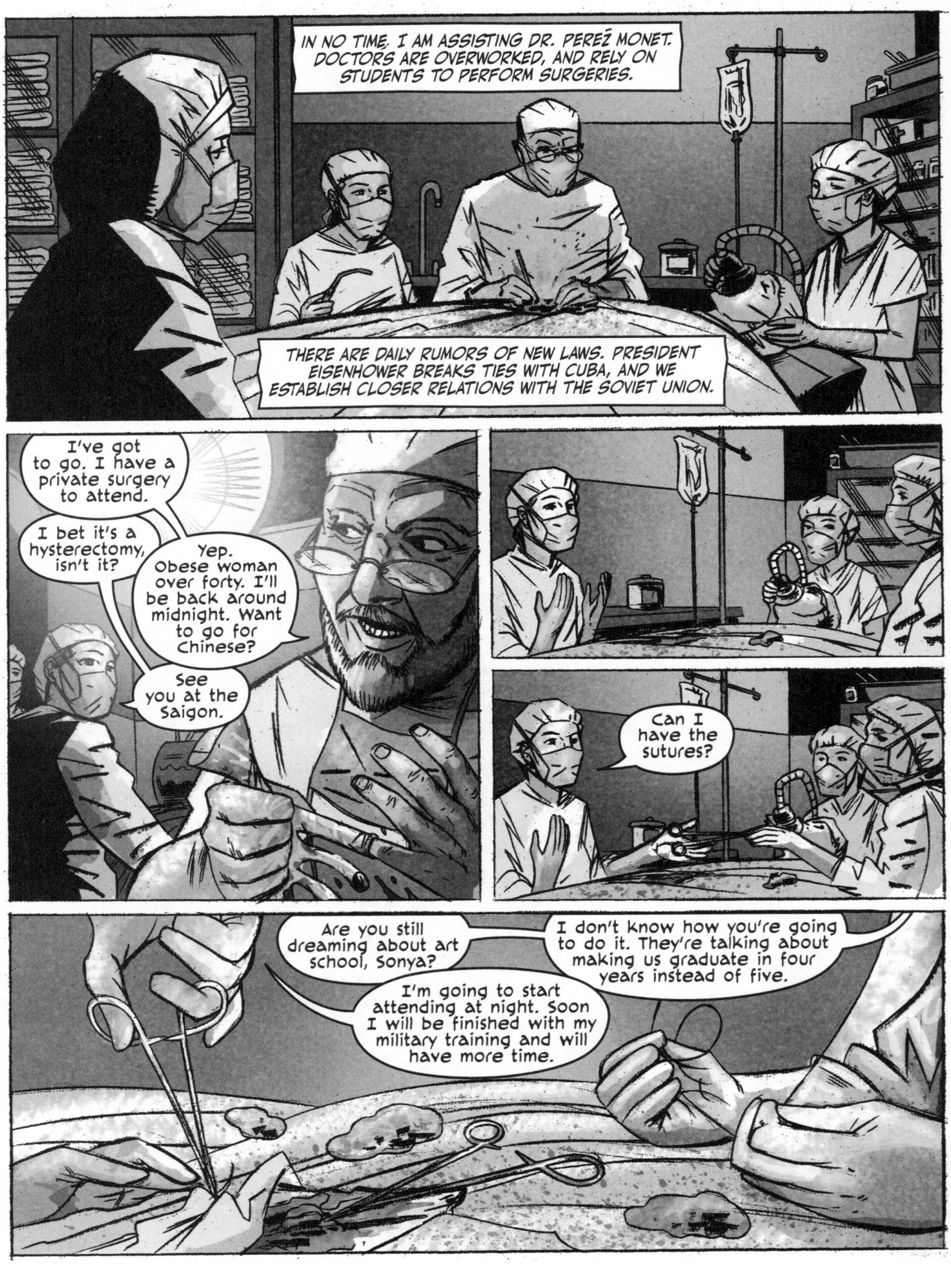
IN NO TIME, I AM ASSISTING DR. PEREŽ MONET. DOCTORS ARE OVERWORKED, AND RELY ON STUDENTS TO PERFORM SURGERIES.
THERE ARE DAILY RUMORS OF NEW LAWS. PRESIDENT EISENHOWER BREAKS TIES WITH CUBA, AND WE ESTABLISH CLOSER RELATIONS WITH THE SOVIET UNION.
I've got to go. I have a private surgery to attend.
I bet it's a hysterectomy, isn't it?
Yep. Obese woman over forty. I'll be back around midnight. Want to go for Chinese?
See you at the Saigon.
Can I have the sutures?
Are you still dreaming about art school, Sonya?
I don't know how you're going to do it. They're talking about making us graduate in four years instead of five.
I'm going to start attending at night. Soon I will be finished with my military training and will have more time.

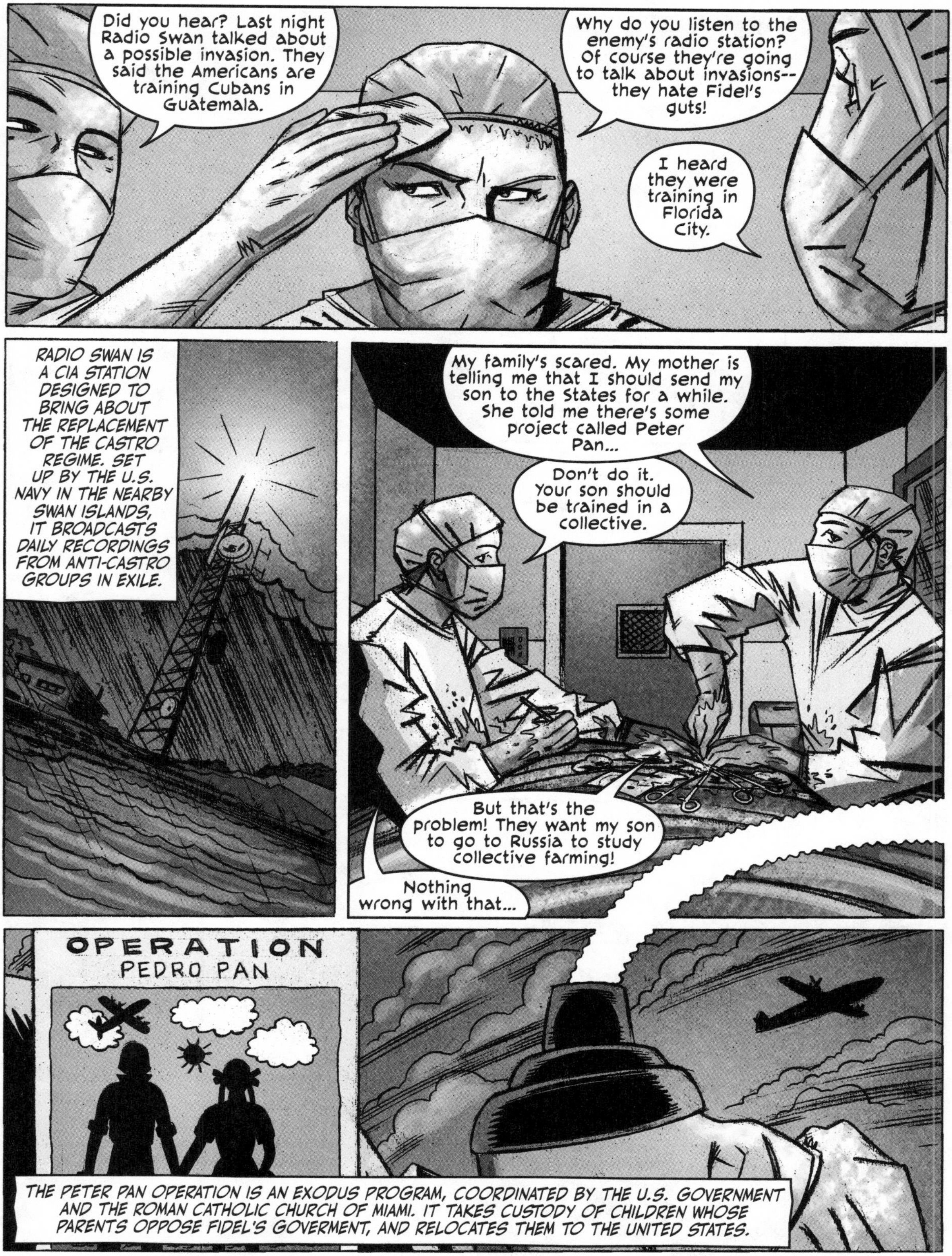

Did you hear? Last night Radio Swan talked about a possible invasion. They said the Americans are training Cubans in Guatemala.
Why do you listen to the enemy's radio station? Of course they're going to talk about invasions--they hate Fidel's guts!
I heard they were training in Florida City.
RADIO SWAN IS A CIA STATION DESIGNED TO BRING ABOUT THE REPLACEMENT OF THE CASTRO REGIME. SET UP BY THE U.S. NAVY IN THE NEARBY SWAN ISLANDS, IT BROADCASTS DAILY RECORDINGS FROM ANTI-CASTRO GROUPS IN EXILE.
My family's scared. My mother is telling me that I should send my son to the States for a while. She told me there's some project called Peter Pan...
Don't do it. Your son should be trained in a collective.
But that's the problem! They want my son to go to Russia to study collective farming!
Nothing wrong with that...
OPERATION
PEDRO PAN
THE PETER PAN OPERATION IS AN EXODUS PROGRAM, COORDINATED BY THE U.S. GOVERNMENT AND THE ROMAN CATHOLIC CHURCH OF MIAMI. IT TAKES CUSTODY OF CHILDREN WHOSE PARENTS OPPOSE FIDEL'S GOVERMENT, AND RELOCATES THEM TO THE UNITED STATES.

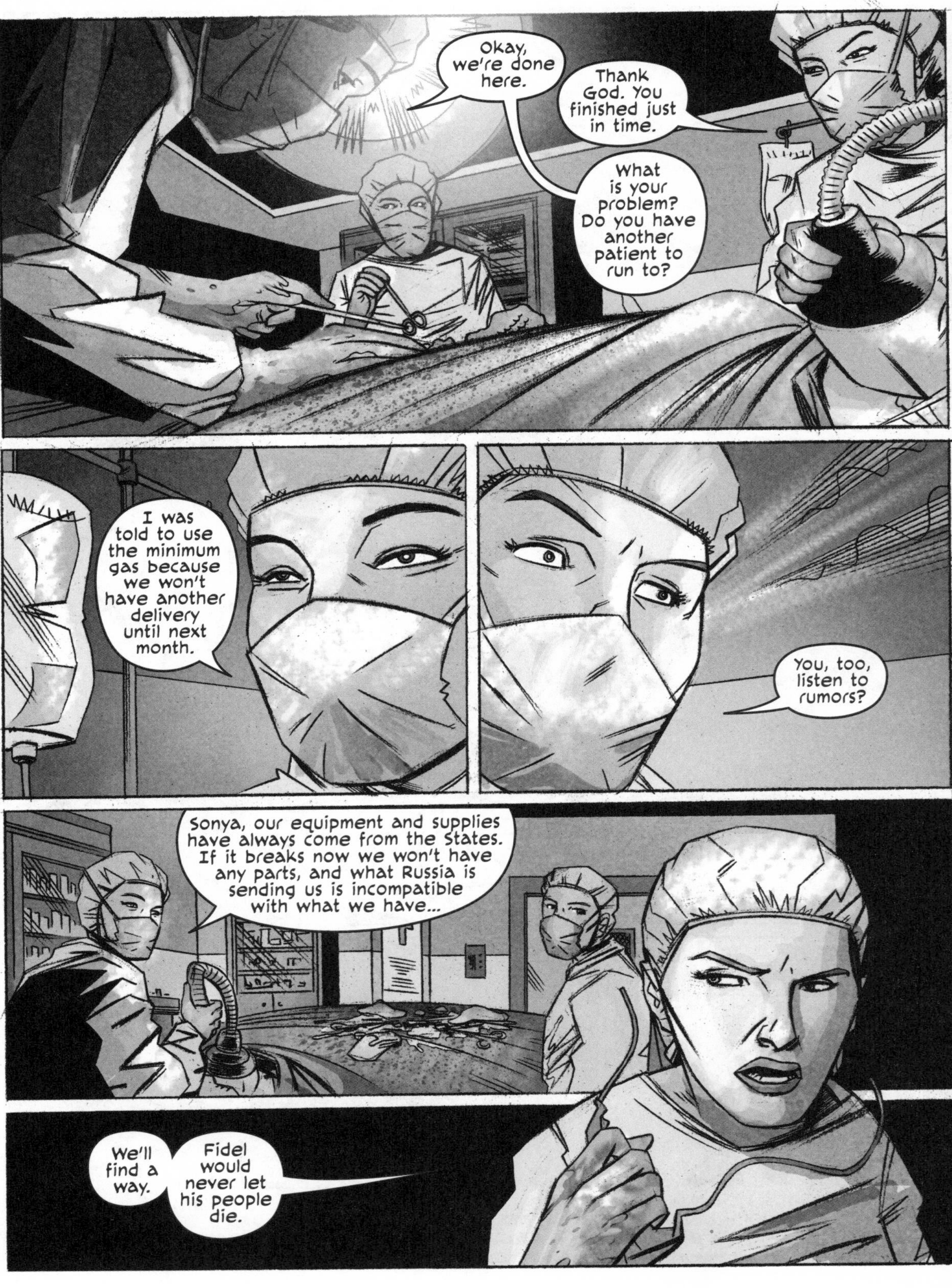
Okay, we're done here.
Thank God. You finished just in time.
What is your problem? Do you have another patient to run to?
I was told to use the minimum gas because we won't have another delivery until next month.
You, too, listen to rumors?
Sonya, our equipment and supplies have always come from the States. If it breaks now we won't have any parts, and what Russia is sending us is incompatible with what we have...
We'll find a way.
Fidel would never let his people die.

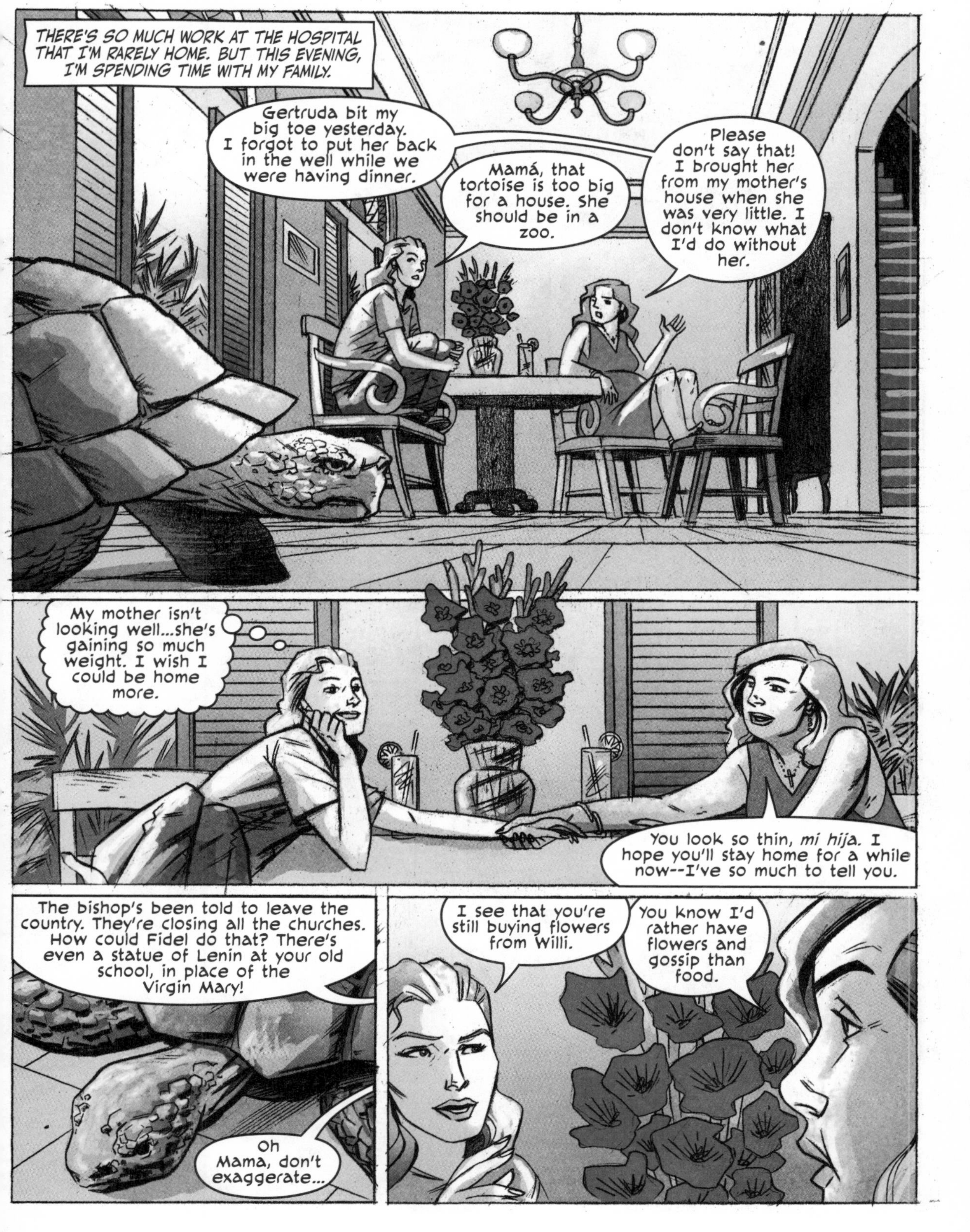
THERE'S SO MUCH WORK AT THE HOSPITAL THAT I'M RARELY HOME. BUT THIS EVENING, I'M SPENDING TIME WITH MY FAMILY.
Gertruda bit my big toe yesterday. I forgot to put her back in the well while we were having dinner.
Mamá, that tortoise is too big for a house. She should be in a zoo.
Please don't say that! I brought her from my mother's house when she was very little. I don't know what I'd do without her.
My mother isn't looking well...she's gaining so much weight. I wish I could be home more.
You look so thin, *mi hija.* I hope you'll stay home for a while now--I've so much to tell you.
The bishop's been told to leave the country. They're closing all the churches. How could Fidel do that? There's even a statue of Lenin at your old school, in place of the Virgin Mary!
Oh Mama, don't exaggerate...
I see that you're still buying flowers from Willi.
You know I'd rather have flowers and gossip than food.

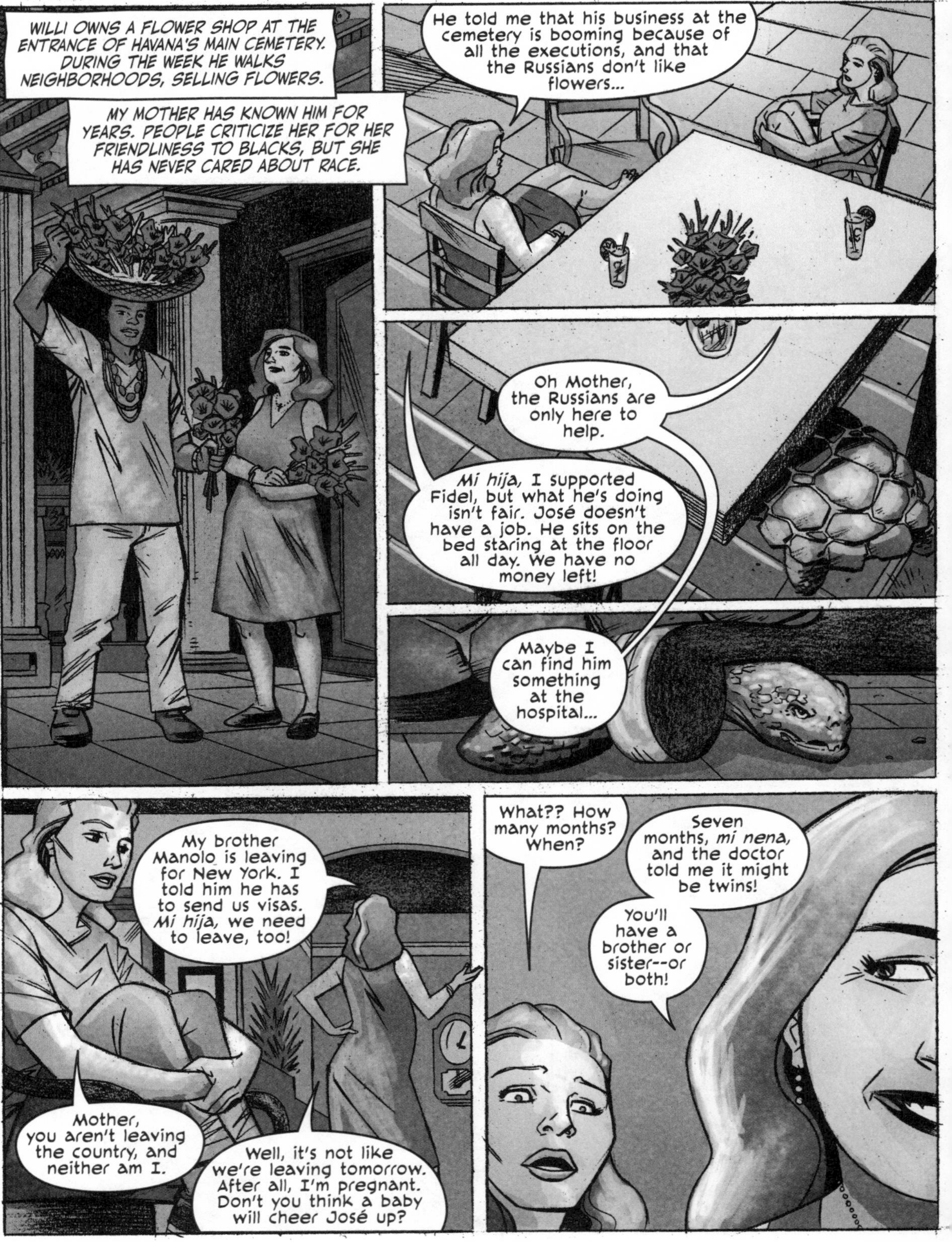
WILLI OWNS A FLOWER SHOP AT THE ENTRANCE OF HAVANA'S MAIN CEMETERY. DURING THE WEEK HE WALKS NEIGHBORHOODS, SELLING FLOWERS.
MY MOTHER HAS KNOWN HIM FOR YEARS. PEOPLE CRITICIZE HER FOR HER FRIENDLINESS TO BLACKS, BUT SHE HAS NEVER CARED ABOUT RACE.
He told me that his business at the cemetery is booming because of all the executions, and that the Russians don't like flowers...
Oh Mother, the Russians are only here to help.
Mi hija, I supported Fidel, but what he's doing isn't fair. José doesn't have a job. He sits on the bed staring at the floor all day. We have no money left!
Maybe I can find him something at the hospital...
My brother Manolo is leaving for New York. I told him he has to send us visas. *Mi hija,* we need to leave, too!
Mother, you aren't leaving the country, and neither am I.
Well, it's not like we're leaving tomorrow. After all, I'm pregnant. Don't you think a baby will cheer José up?
What?? How many months? When?
Seven months, *mi nena,* and the doctor told me it might be twins!
You'll have a brother or sister--or both!

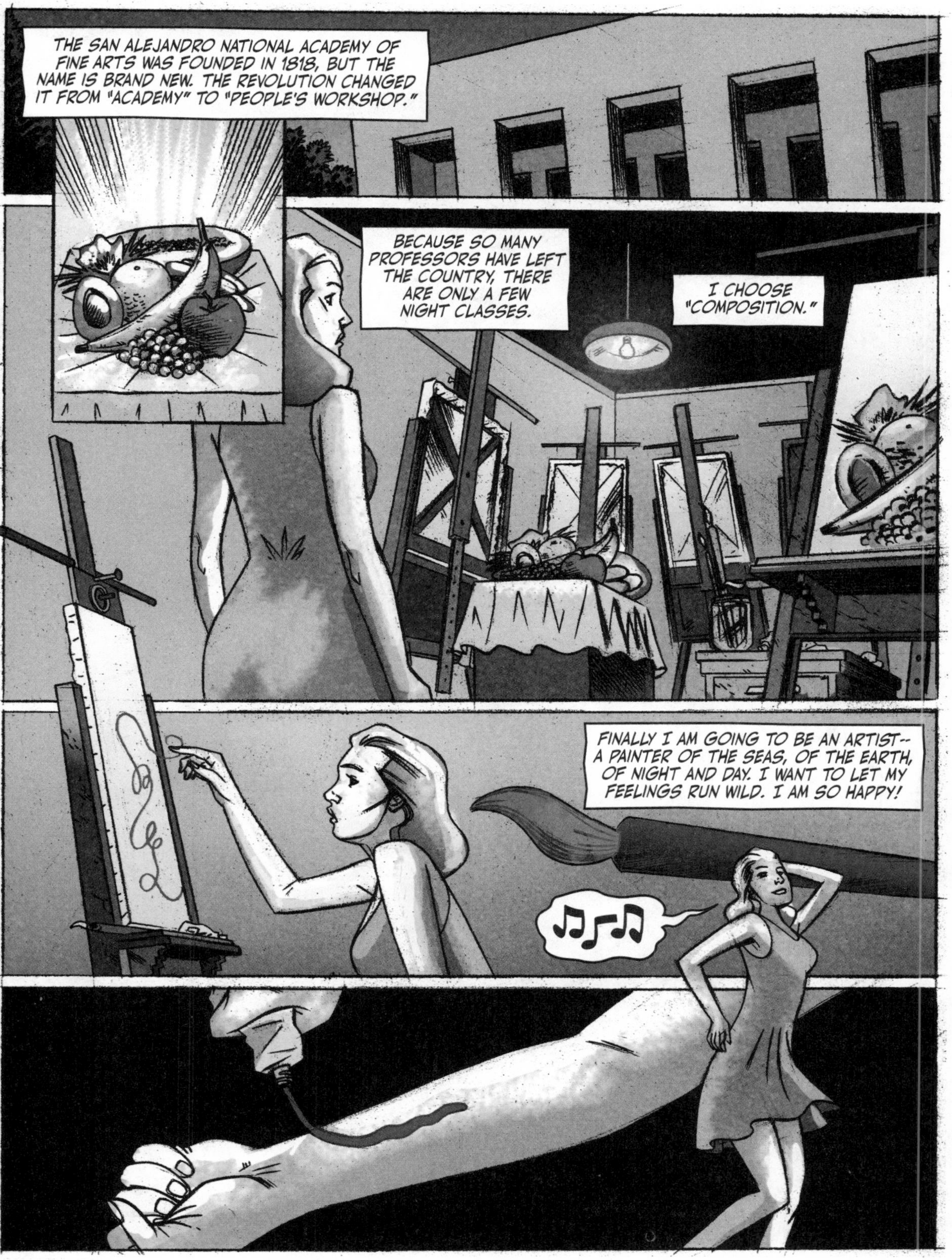
THE SAN ALEJANDRO NATIONAL ACADEMY OF FINE ARTS WAS FOUNDED IN 1818, BUT THE NAME IS BRAND NEW. THE REVOLUTION CHANGED IT FROM "ACADEMY" TO "PEOPLE'S WORKSHOP."
BECAUSE SO MANY PROFESSORS HAVE LEFT THE COUNTRY, THERE ARE ONLY A FEW NIGHT CLASSES.
I CHOOSE "COMPOSITION."
FINALLY I AM GOING TO BE AN ARTIST-- A PAINTER OF THE SEAS, OF THE EARTH, OF NIGHT AND DAY. I WANT TO LET MY FEELINGS RUN WILD. I AM SO HAPPY!

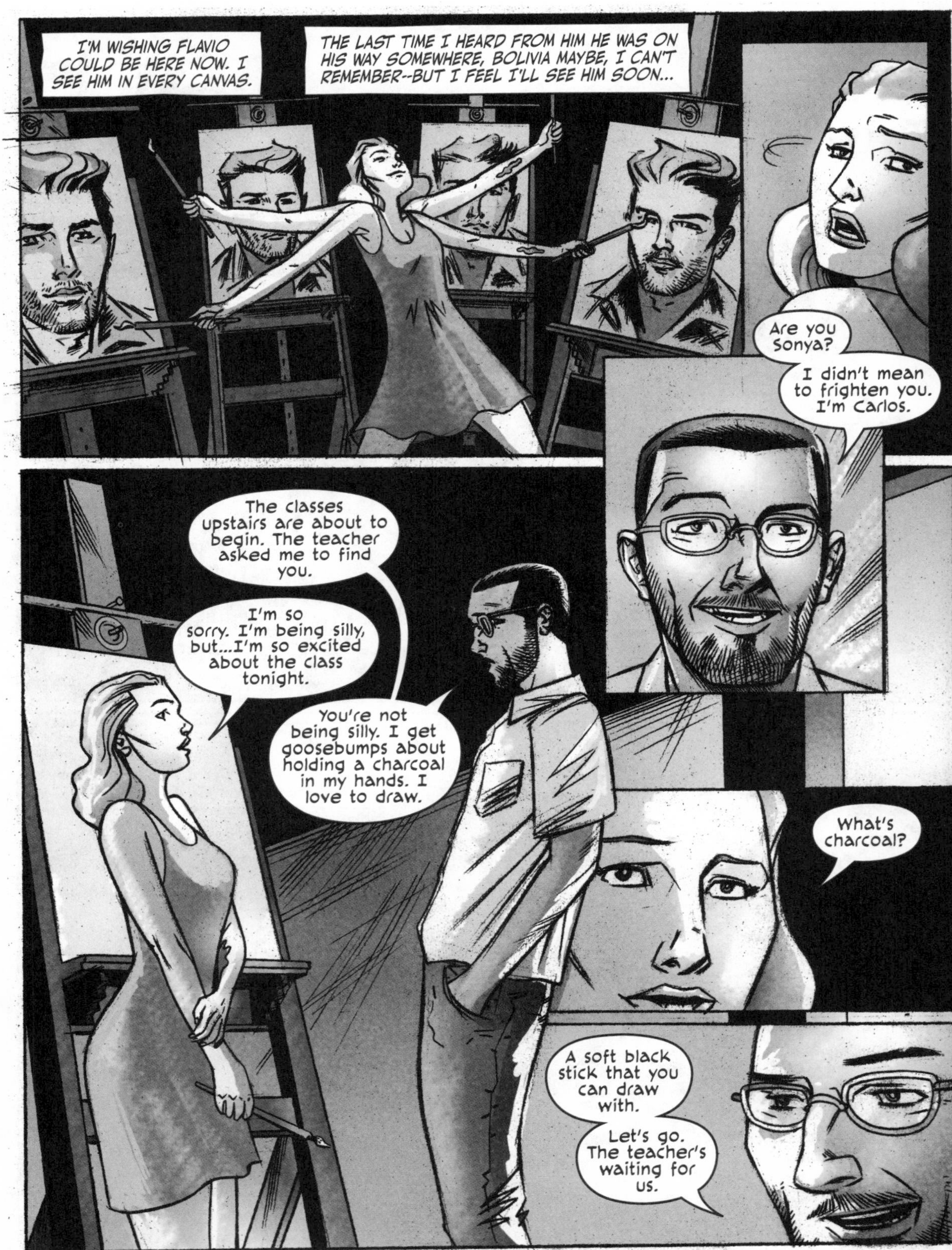
I'M WISHING FLAVIO COULD BE HERE NOW. I SEE HIM IN EVERY CANVAS.
THE LAST TIME I HEARD FROM HIM HE WAS ON HIS WAY SOMEWHERE, BOLIVIA MAYBE, I CAN'T REMEMBER--BUT I FEEL I'LL SEE HIM SOON...
Are you Sonya?
I didn't mean to frighten you. I'm Carlos.
The classes upstairs are about to begin. The teacher asked me to find you.
I'm so sorry. I'm being silly, but...I'm so excited about the class tonight.
You're not being silly. I get goosebumps about holding a charcoal in my hands. I love to draw.
What's charcoal?
A soft black stick that you can draw with.
Let's go. The teacher's waiting for us.

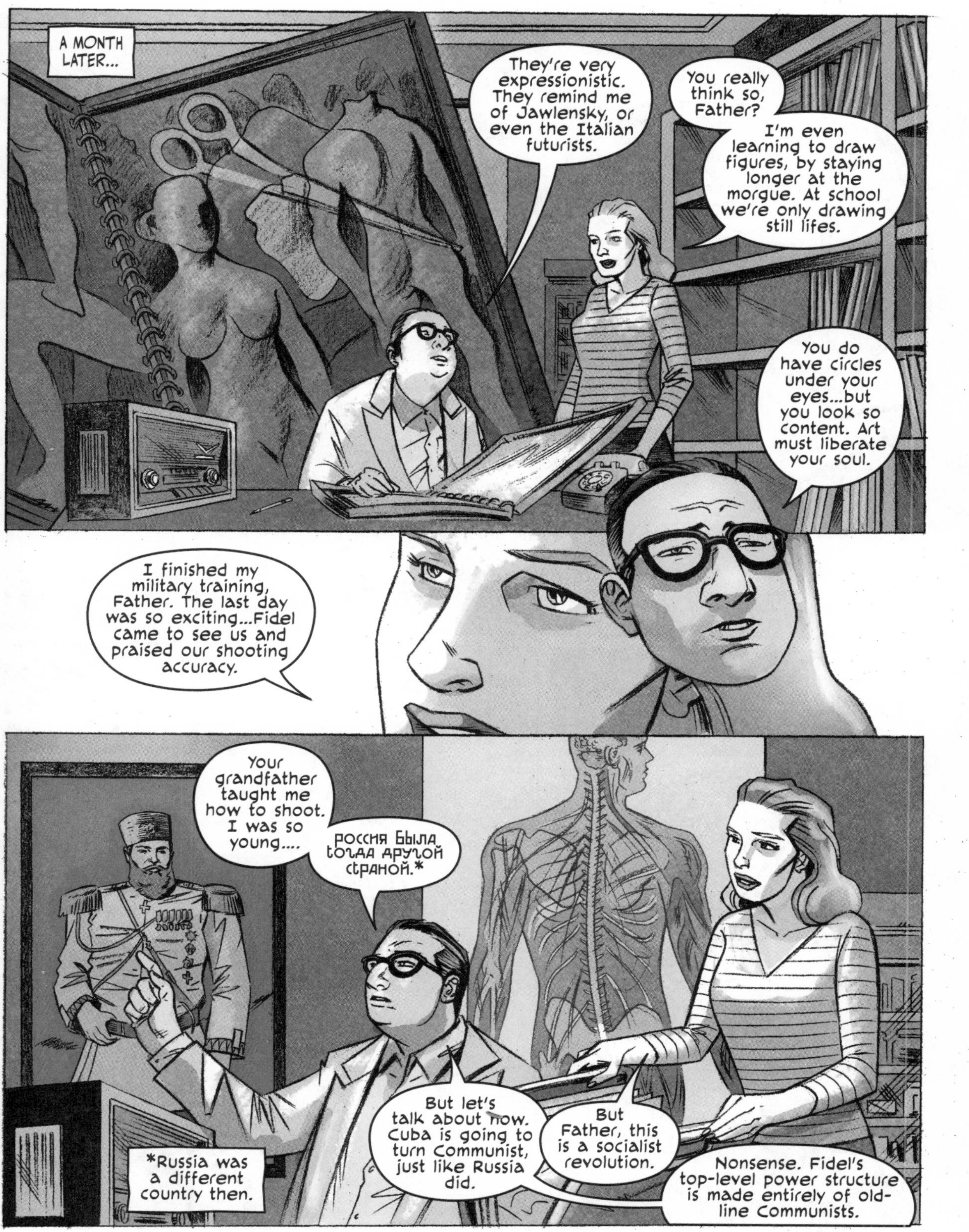
A MONTH LATER...
They're very expressionistic. They remind me of Jawlensky, or even the Italian futurists.
You really think so, Father?
I'm even learning to draw figures, by staying longer at the morgue. At school we're only drawing still lifes.
You do have circles under your eyes...but you look so content. Art must liberate your soul.
I finished my military training, Father. The last day was so exciting...Fidel came to see us and praised our shooting accuracy.
Your grandfather taught me how to shoot. I was so young....
россия была тогда другой страной.*
*Russia was a different country then.
But let's talk about now. Cuba is going to turn Communist, just like Russia did.
But Father, this is a socialist revolution.
Nonsense. Fidel's top-level power structure is made entirely of old-line Communists.

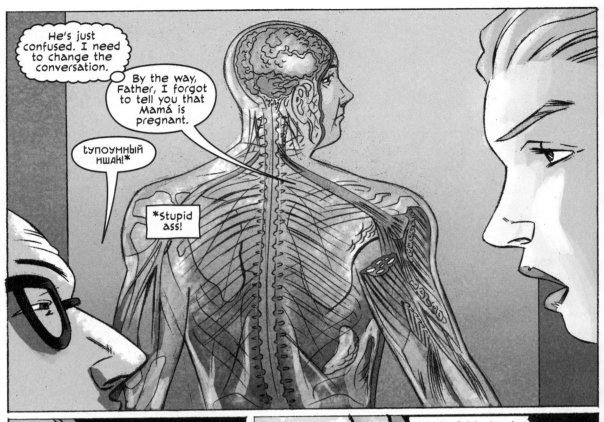

He's just confused. I need to change the conversation.

By the way, Father, I forgot to tell you that Mamá is pregnant.

ТУПОУМНЫЙ ИШАК!*

*Stupid ass!

...What did you say?

That your mother has a strange way of resolving situations.

He's right about my mother, but not about us becoming a communist country.

My mother may be irrational at times, but my father can be so preposterous!

I've got to go, Father...

I'm very proud of you...but don't be a socialist hero.

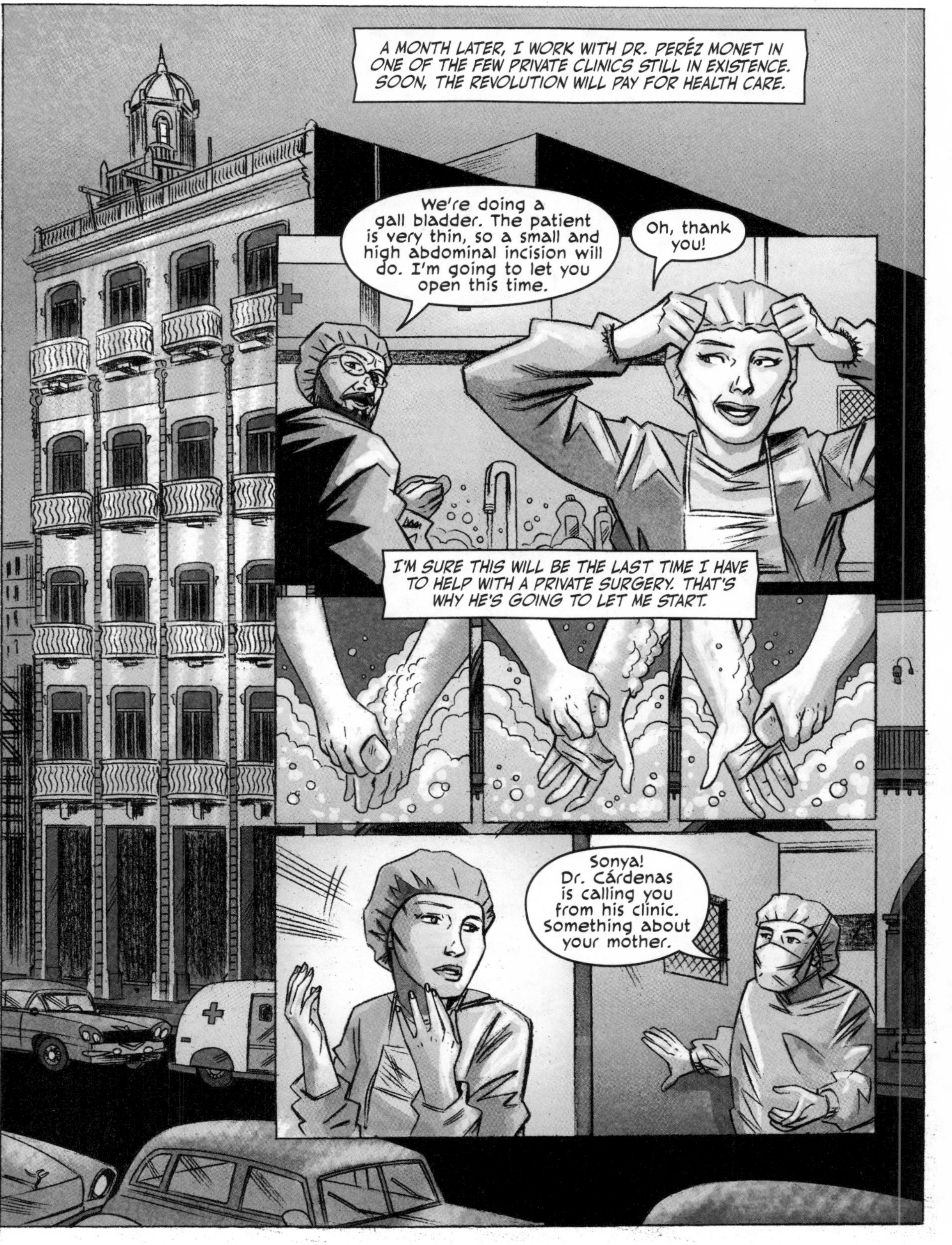
A MONTH LATER, I WORK WITH DR. PERÉZ MONET IN ONE OF THE FEW PRIVATE CLINICS STILL IN EXISTENCE. SOON, THE REVOLUTION WILL PAY FOR HEALTH CARE.
We're doing a gall bladder. The patient is very thin, so a small and high abdominal incision will do. I'm going to let you open this time.
Oh, thank you!
I'M SURE THIS WILL BE THE LAST TIME I HAVE TO HELP WITH A PRIVATE SURGERY. THAT'S WHY HE'S GOING TO LET ME START.
Sonya! Dr. Cárdenas is calling you from his clinic. Something about your mother.

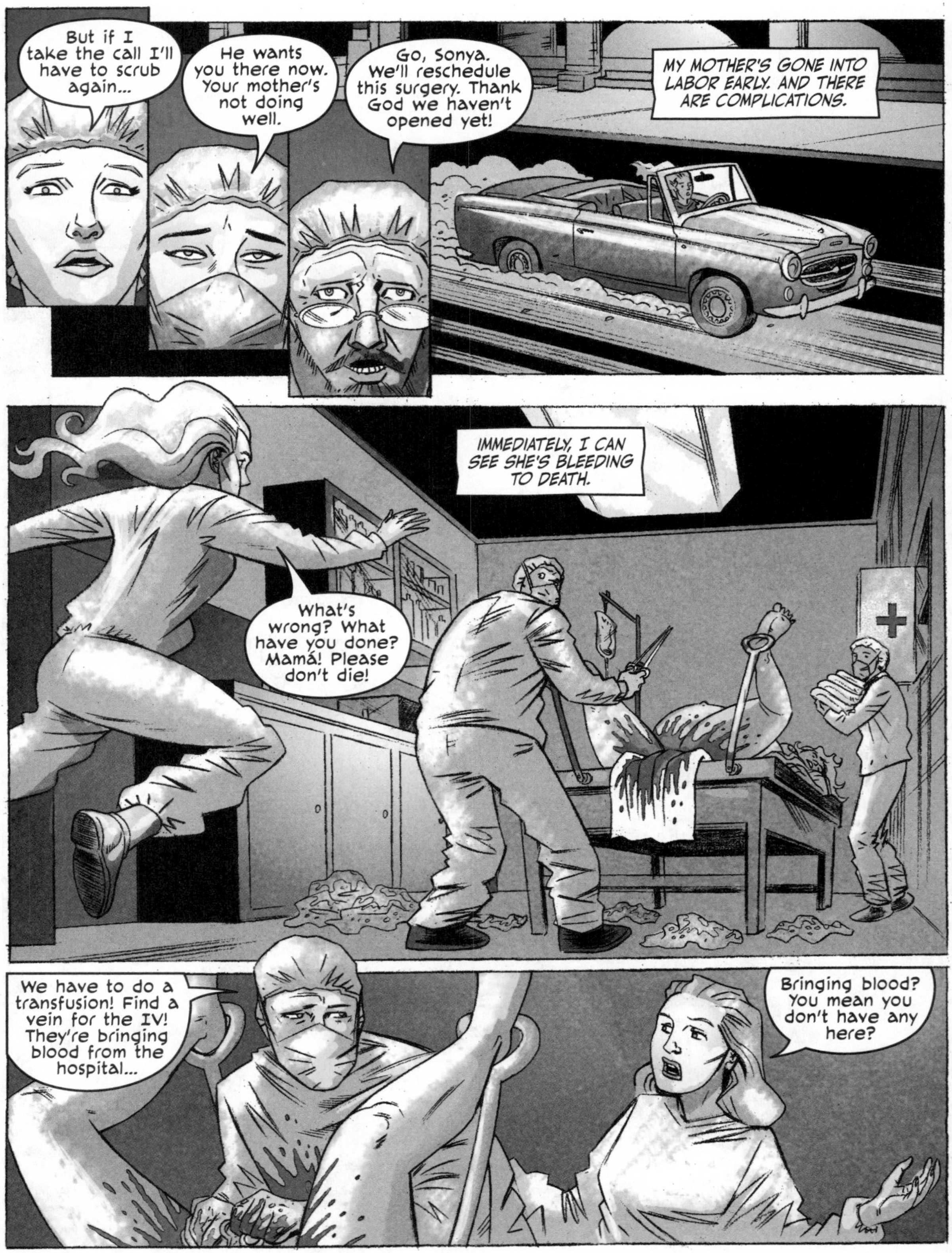
But if I take the call I'll have to scrub again...
He wants you there now. Your mother's not doing well.
Go, Sonya. We'll reschedule this surgery. Thank God we haven't opened yet!
MY MOTHER'S GONE INTO LABOR EARLY. AND THERE ARE COMPLICATIONS.
IMMEDIATELY, I CAN SEE SHE'S BLEEDING TO DEATH.
What's wrong? What have you done? Mamá! Please don't die!
We have to do a transfusion! Find a vein for the IV! They're bringing blood from the hospital...
Bringing blood? You mean you don't have any here?

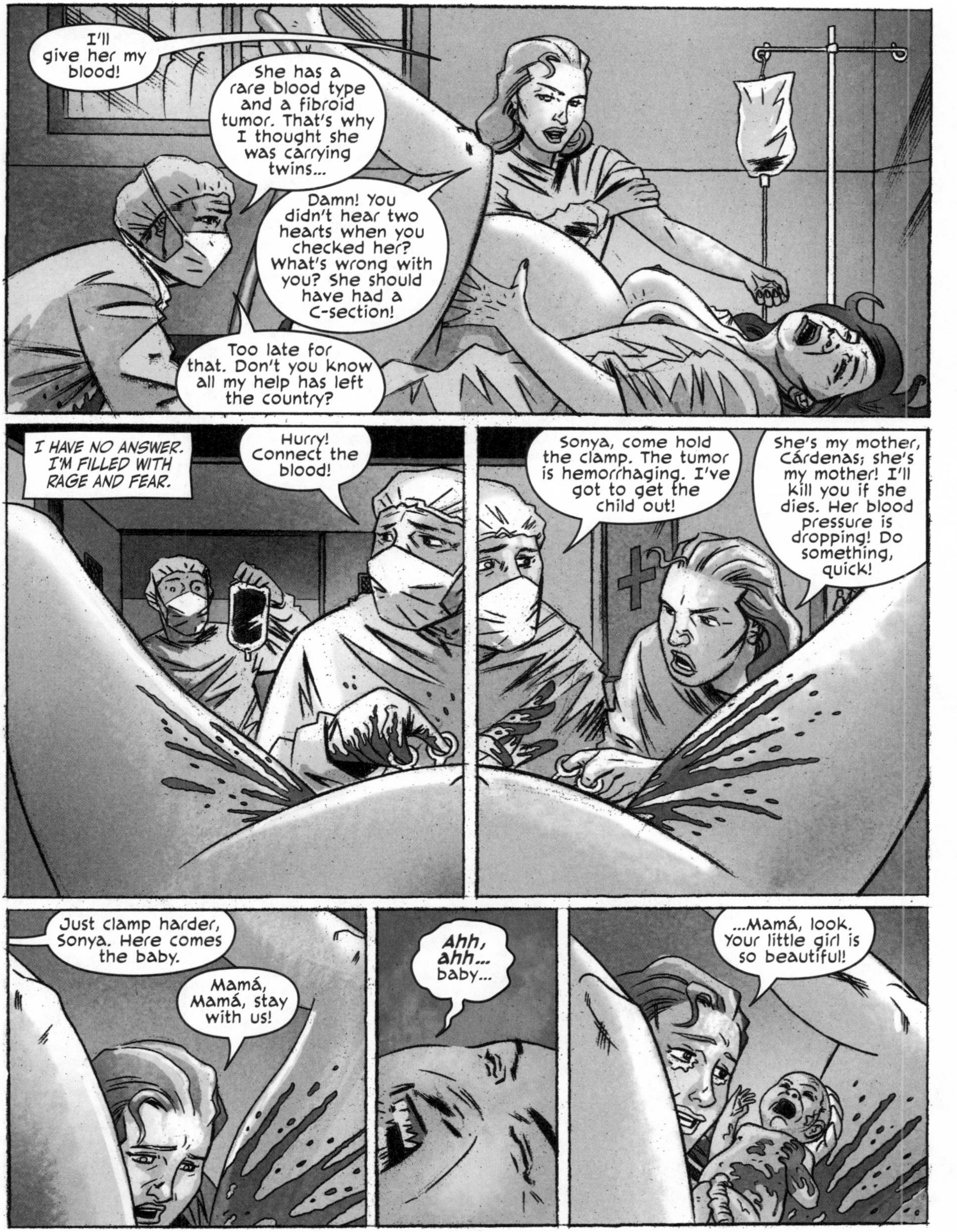
I'll give her my blood!
She has a rare blood type and a fibroid tumor. That's why I thought she was carrying twins...
Damn! You didn't hear two hearts when you checked her? What's wrong with you? She should have had a C-section!
Too late for that. Don't you know all my help has left the country?
I HAVE NO ANSWER. I'M FILLED WITH RAGE AND FEAR.
Hurry! Connect the blood!
Sonya, come hold the clamp. The tumor is hemorrhaging. I've got to get the child out!
She's my mother, Cárdenas; she's my mother! I'll kill you if she dies. Her blood pressure is dropping! Do something, quick!
Just clamp harder, Sonya. Here comes the baby.
Mamá, Mamá, stay with us!
Ahh, ahh... baby...
...Mamá, look. Your little girl is so beautiful!

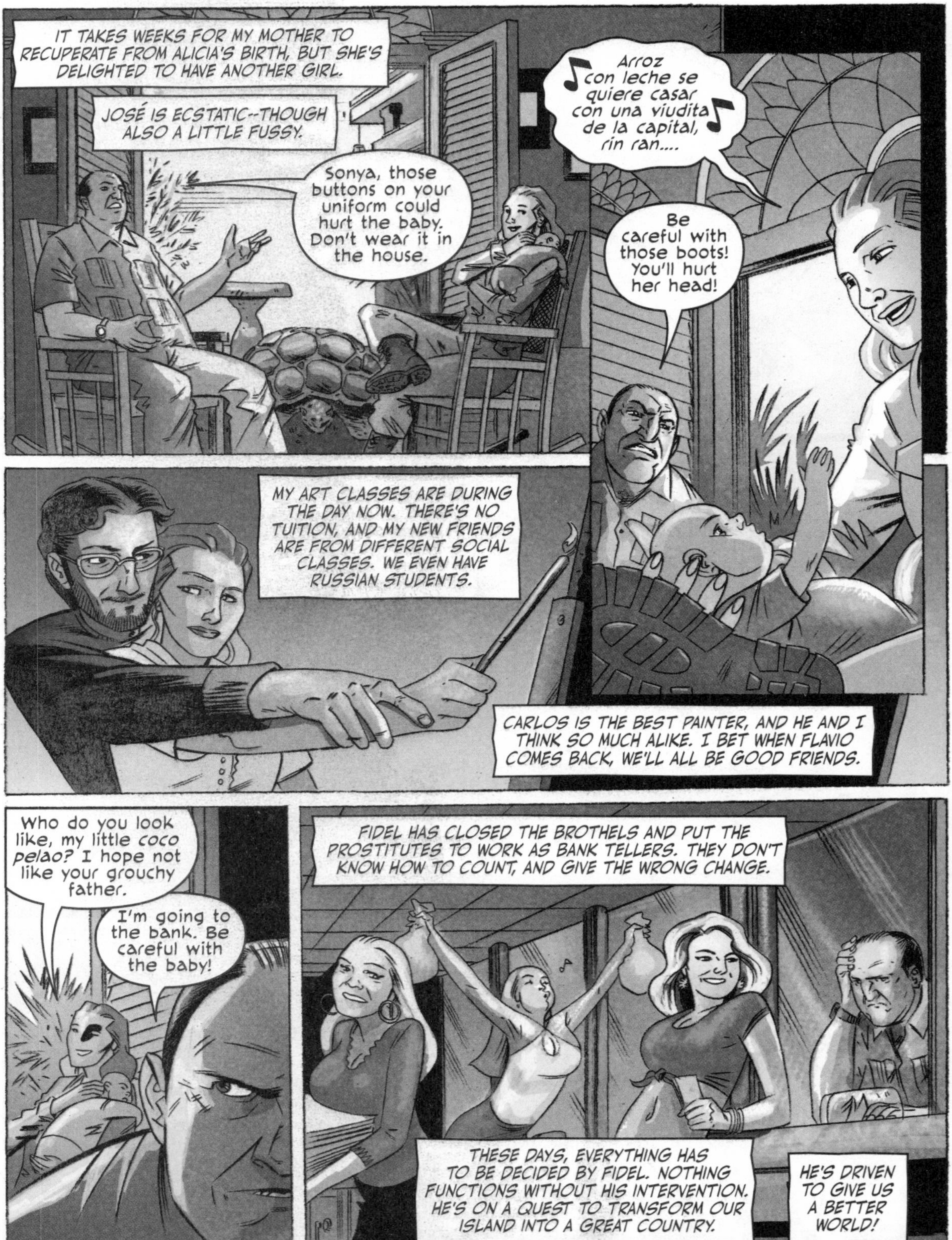

IT TAKES WEEKS FOR MY MOTHER TO RECUPERATE FROM ALICIA'S BIRTH, BUT SHE'S DELIGHTED TO HAVE ANOTHER GIRL.
JOSÉ IS ECSTATIC--THOUGH ALSO A LITTLE FUSSY.
Sonya, those buttons on your uniform could hurt the baby. Don't wear it in the house.
Arroz con leche se quiere casar con una viudita de la capital, rin ran....
Be careful with those boots! You'll hurt her head!
MY ART CLASSES ARE DURING THE DAY NOW. THERE'S NO TUITION, AND MY NEW FRIENDS ARE FROM DIFFERENT SOCIAL CLASSES. WE EVEN HAVE RUSSIAN STUDENTS.
CARLOS IS THE BEST PAINTER, AND HE AND I THINK SO MUCH ALIKE. I BET WHEN FLAVIO COMES BACK, WE'LL ALL BE GOOD FRIENDS.
Who do you look like, my little coco pelao? I hope not like your grouchy father.
I'm going to the bank. Be careful with the baby!
FIDEL HAS CLOSED THE BROTHELS AND PUT THE PROSTITUTES TO WORK AS BANK TELLERS. THEY DON'T KNOW HOW TO COUNT, AND GIVE THE WRONG CHANGE.
THESE DAYS, EVERYTHING HAS TO BE DECIDED BY FIDEL. NOTHING FUNCTIONS WITHOUT HIS INTERVENTION. HE'S ON A QUEST TO TRANSFORM OUR ISLAND INTO A GREAT COUNTRY.
HE'S DRIVEN TO GIVE US A BETTER WORLD!

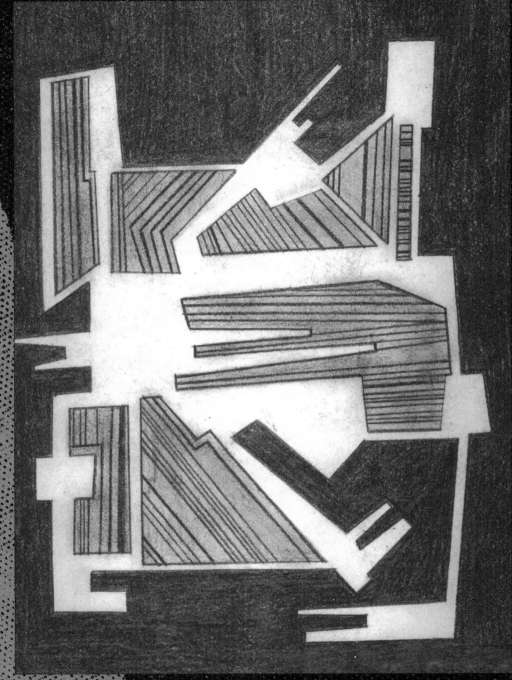

PART TWO

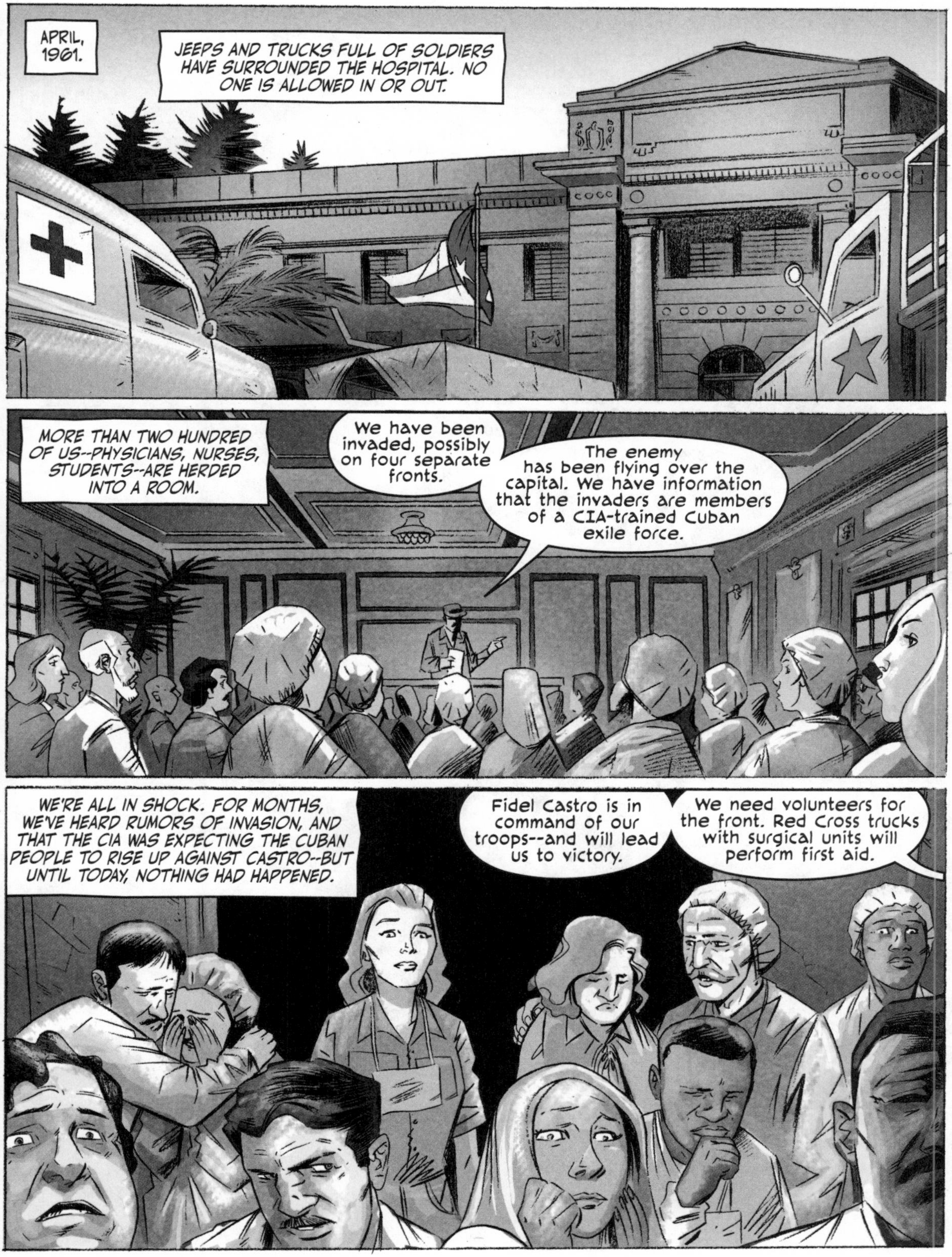
APRIL, 1961.
JEEPS AND TRUCKS FULL OF SOLDIERS HAVE SURROUNDED THE HOSPITAL. NO ONE IS ALLOWED IN OR OUT.
MORE THAN TWO HUNDRED OF US--PHYSICIANS, NURSES, STUDENTS--ARE HERDED INTO A ROOM.
We have been invaded, possibly on four separate fronts.
The enemy has been flying over the capital. We have information that the invaders are members of a CIA-trained Cuban exile force.
WE'RE ALL IN SHOCK. FOR MONTHS, WE'VE HEARD RUMORS OF INVASION, AND THAT THE CIA WAS EXPECTING THE CUBAN PEOPLE TO RISE UP AGAINST CASTRO--BUT UNTIL TODAY, NOTHING HAD HAPPENED.
Fidel Castro is in command of our troops--and will lead us to victory.
We need volunteers for the front. Red Cross trucks with surgical units will perform first aid.

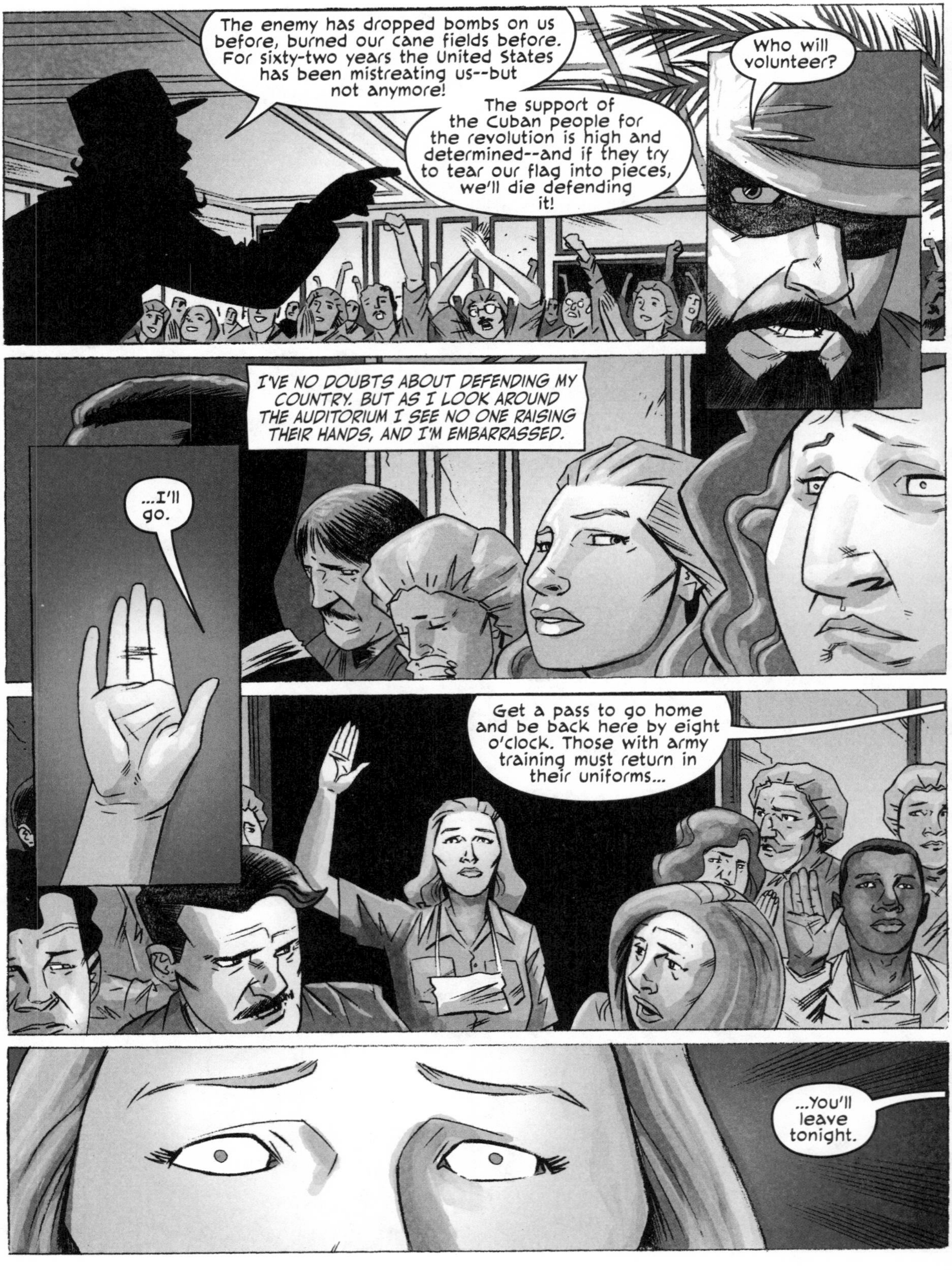
The enemy has dropped bombs on us before, burned our cane fields before. For sixty-two years the United States has been mistreating us--but not anymore!
The support of the Cuban people for the revolution is high and determined--and if they try to tear our flag into pieces, we'll die defending it!
Who will volunteer?
I'VE NO DOUBTS ABOUT DEFENDING MY COUNTRY. BUT AS I LOOK AROUND THE AUDITORIUM I SEE NO ONE RAISING THEIR HANDS, AND I'M EMBARRASSED.
...I'll go.
Get a pass to go home and be back here by eight o'clock. Those with army training must return in their uniforms...
...You'll leave tonight.

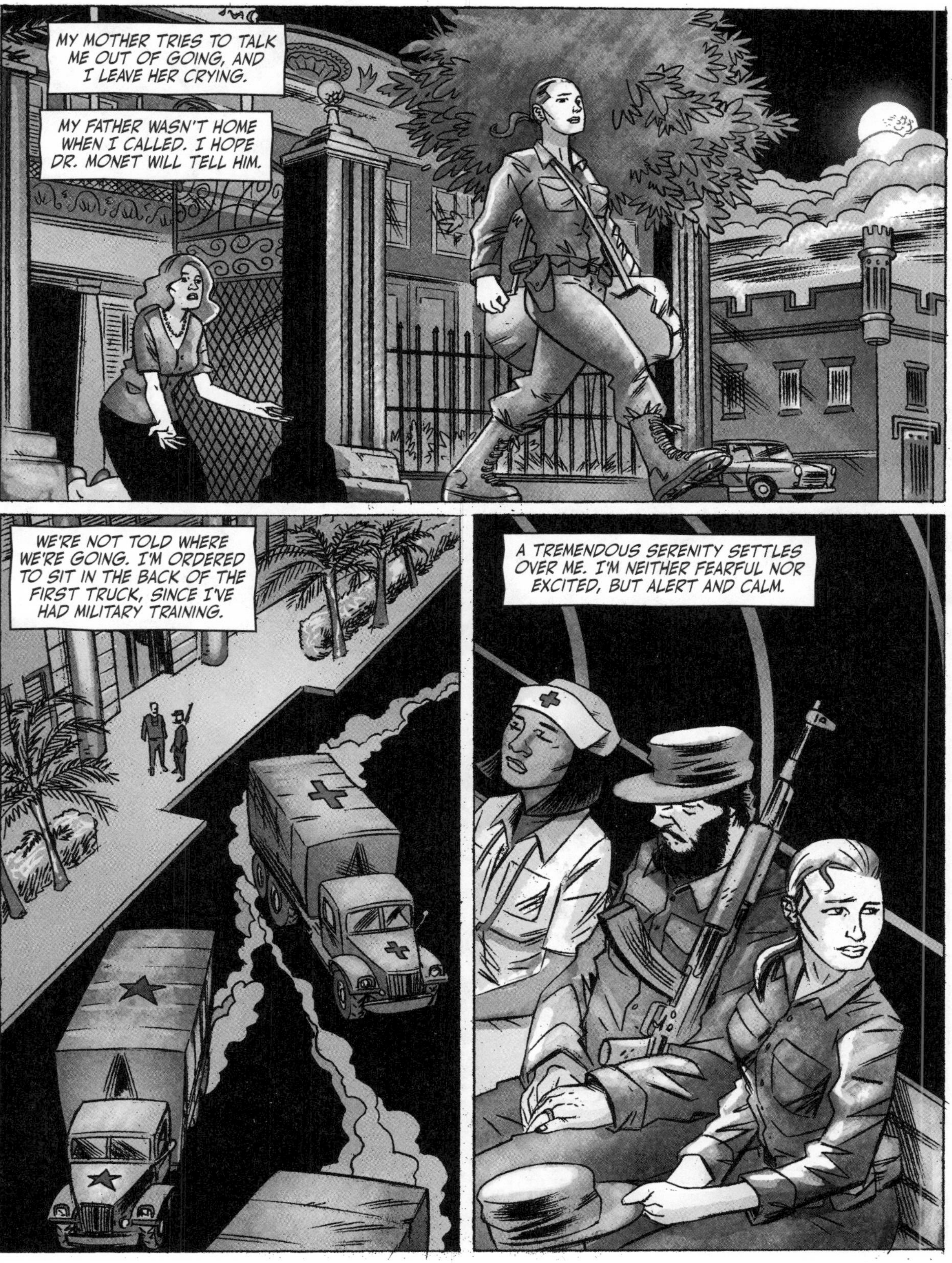
MY MOTHER TRIES TO TALK ME OUT OF GOING, AND I LEAVE HER CRYING.
MY FATHER WASN'T HOME WHEN I CALLED. I HOPE DR. MONET WILL TELL HIM.
WE'RE NOT TOLD WHERE WE'RE GOING. I'M ORDERED TO SIT IN THE BACK OF THE FIRST TRUCK, SINCE I'VE HAD MILITARY TRAINING.
A TREMENDOUS SERENITY SETTLES OVER ME. I'M NEITHER FEARFUL NOR EXCITED, BUT ALERT AND CALM.

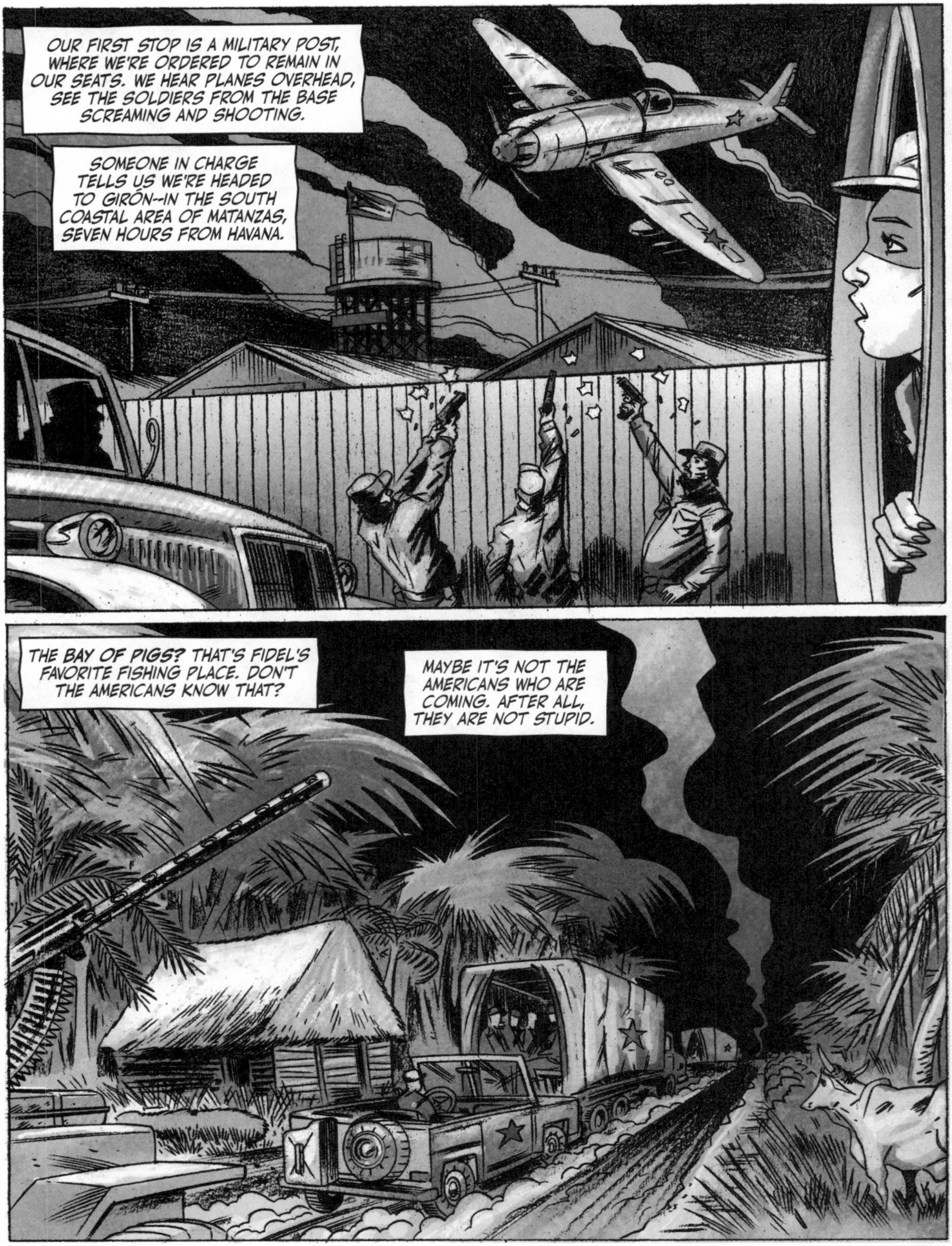
OUR FIRST STOP IS A MILITARY POST, WHERE WE'RE ORDERED TO REMAIN IN OUR SEATS. WE HEAR PLANES OVERHEAD, SEE THE SOLDIERS FROM THE BASE SCREAMING AND SHOOTING.
SOMEONE IN CHARGE TELLS US WE'RE HEADED TO GIRÓN--IN THE SOUTH COASTAL AREA OF MATANZAS, SEVEN HOURS FROM HAVANA.
THE BAY OF PIGS? THAT'S FIDEL'S FAVORITE FISHING PLACE. DON'T THE AMERICANS KNOW THAT?
MAYBE IT'S NOT THE AMERICANS WHO ARE COMING. AFTER ALL, THEY ARE NOT STUPID.

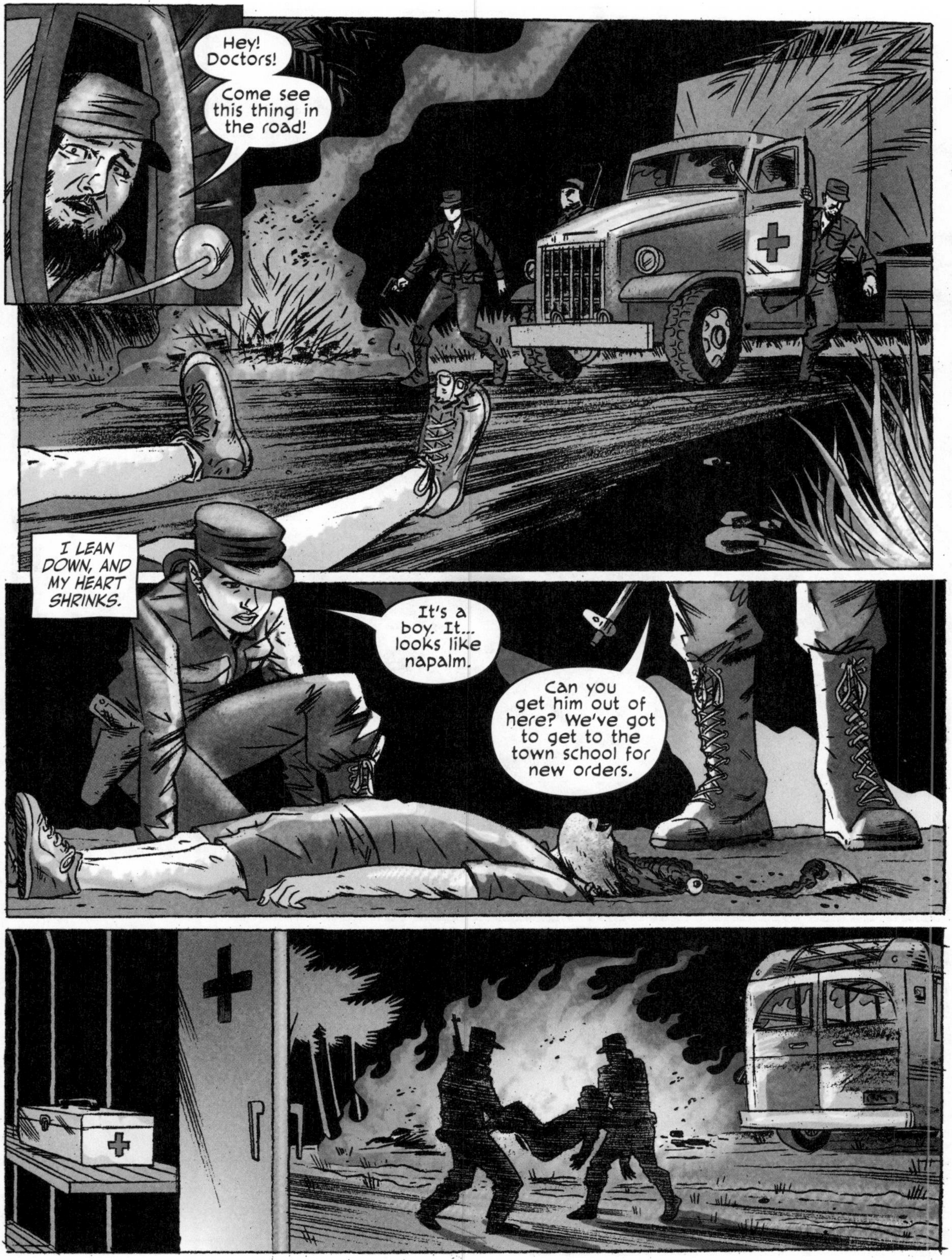
Hey! Doctors!
Come see this thing in the road!
I LEAN DOWN, AND MY HEART SHRINKS.
It's a boy. It... looks like napalm.
Can you get him out of here? We've got to get to the town school for new orders.

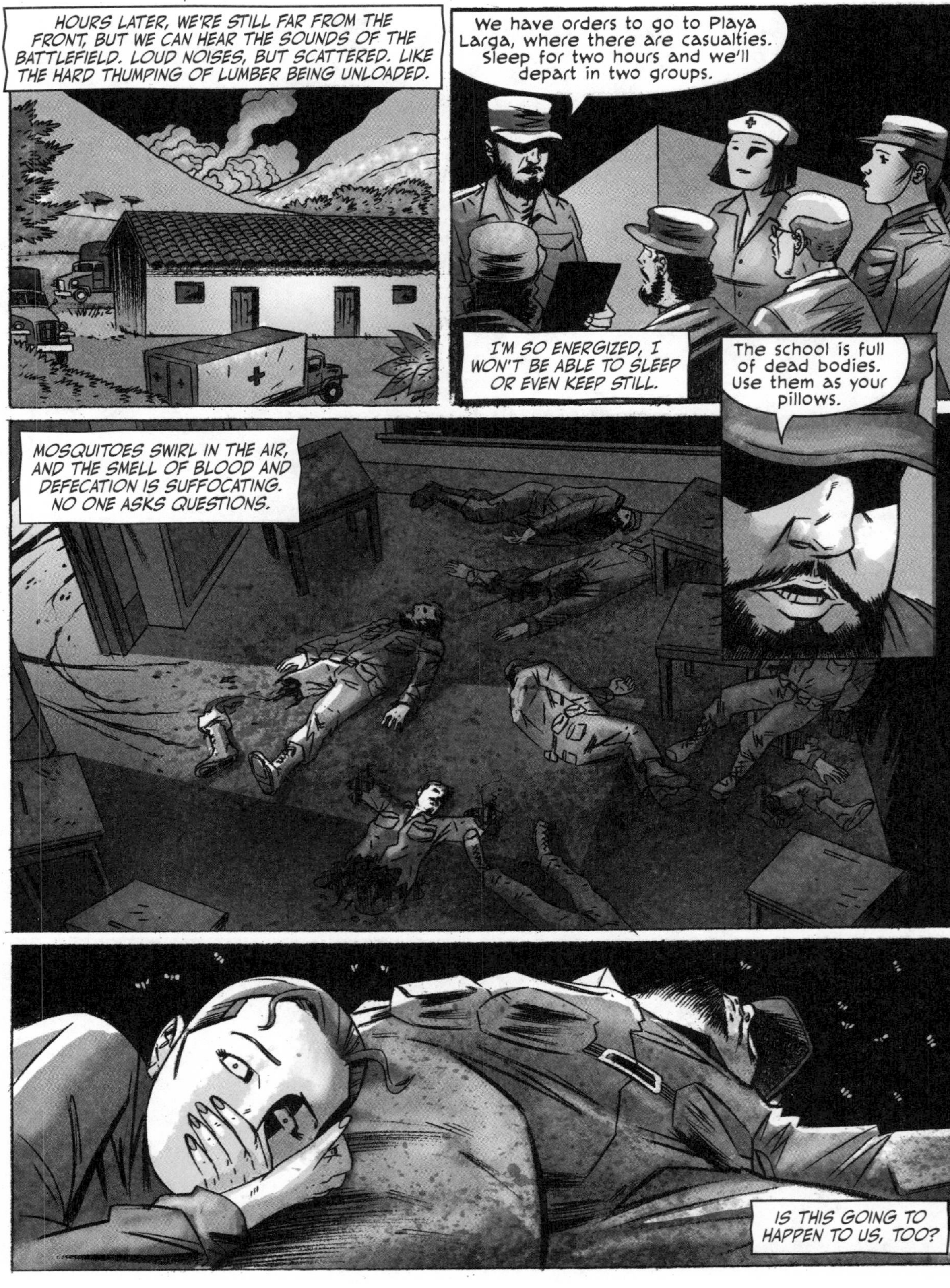
HOURS LATER, WE'RE STILL FAR FROM THE FRONT, BUT WE CAN HEAR THE SOUNDS OF THE BATTLEFIELD. LOUD NOISES, BUT SCATTERED. LIKE THE HARD THUMPING OF LUMBER BEING UNLOADED.
We have orders to go to Playa Larga, where there are casualties. Sleep for two hours and we'll depart in two groups.
I'M SO ENERGIZED, I WON'T BE ABLE TO SLEEP OR EVEN KEEP STILL.
The school is full of dead bodies. Use them as your pillows.
MOSQUITOES SWIRL IN THE AIR, AND THE SMELL OF BLOOD AND DEFECATION IS SUFFOCATING. NO ONE ASKS QUESTIONS.
IS THIS GOING TO HAPPEN TO US, TOO?

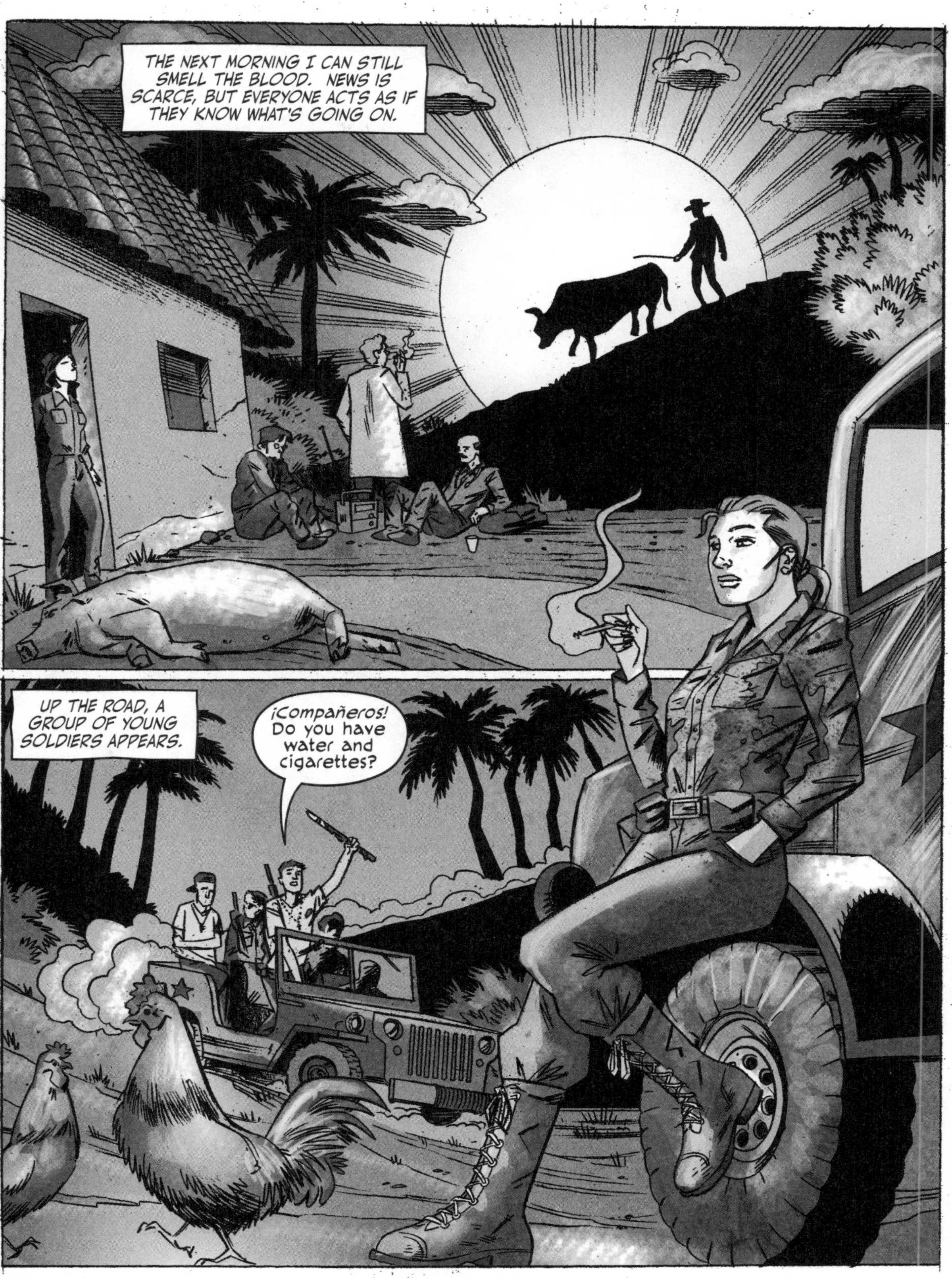
THE NEXT MORNING I CAN STILL SMELL THE BLOOD. NEWS IS SCARCE, BUT EVERYONE ACTS AS IF THEY KNOW WHAT'S GOING ON.
UP THE ROAD, A GROUP OF YOUNG SOLDIERS APPEARS.
¡Compañeros! Do you have water and cigarettes?

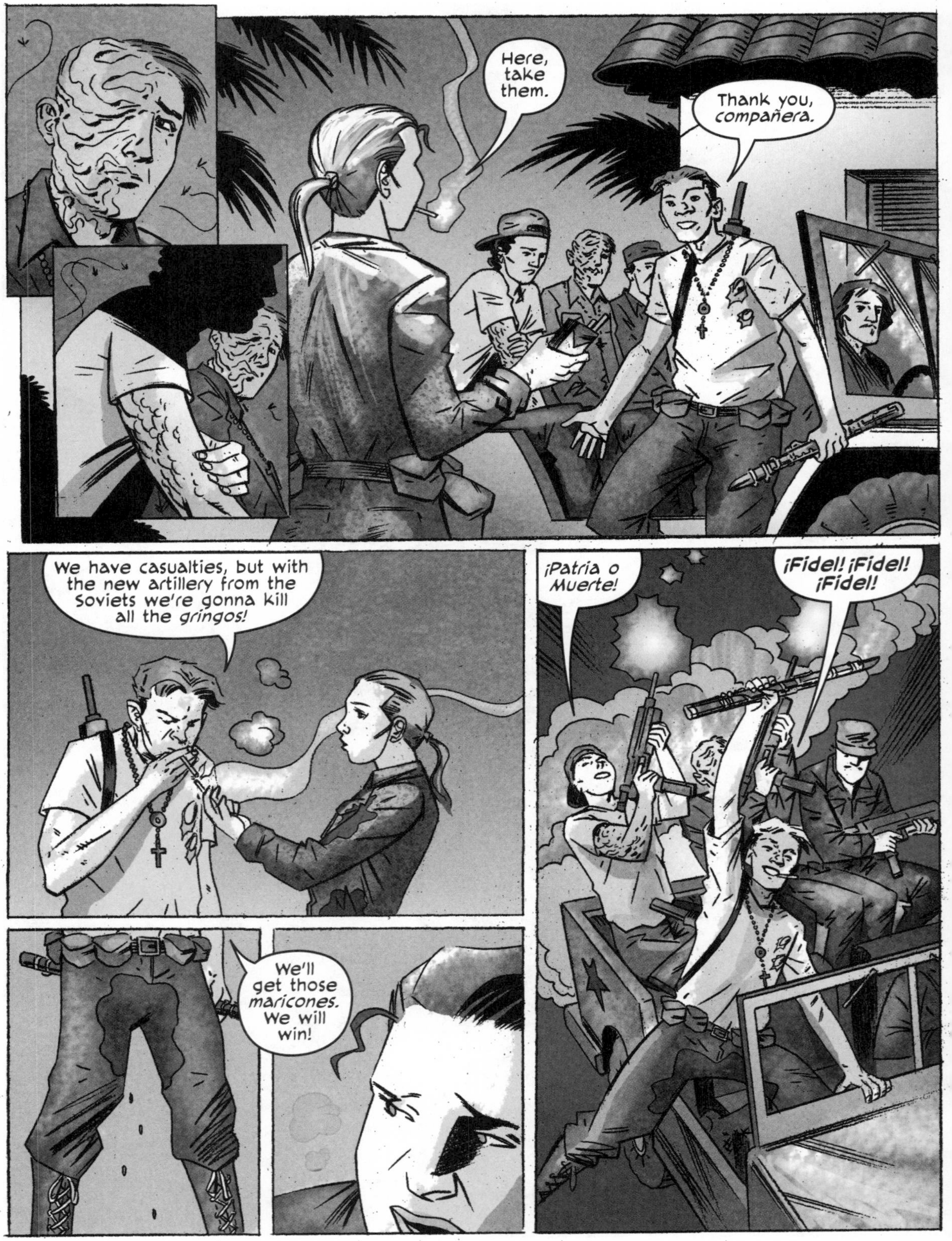

Here, take them.
Thank you, *compañera.*
We have casualties, but with the new artillery from the Soviets we're gonna kill all the *gringos!*
We'll get those *maricones.* We will win!
¡Patria o Muerte!
¡Fidel! ¡Fidel! ¡Fidel!

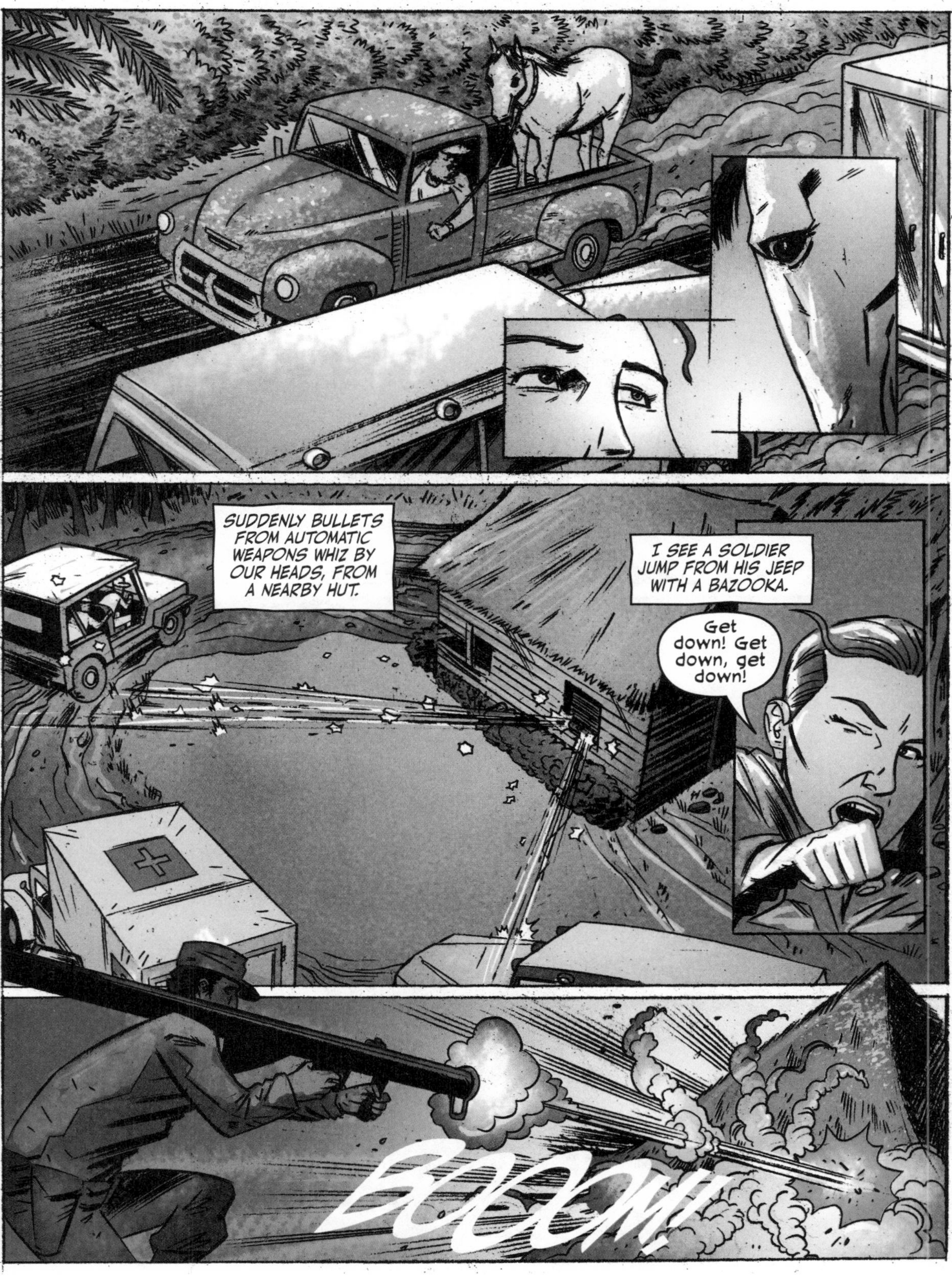
SUDDENLY BULLETS FROM AUTOMATIC WEAPONS WHIZ BY OUR HEADS, FROM A NEARBY HUT.
I SEE A SOLDIER JUMP FROM HIS JEEP WITH A BAZOOKA.
Get down! Get down, get down!
BOOOM!

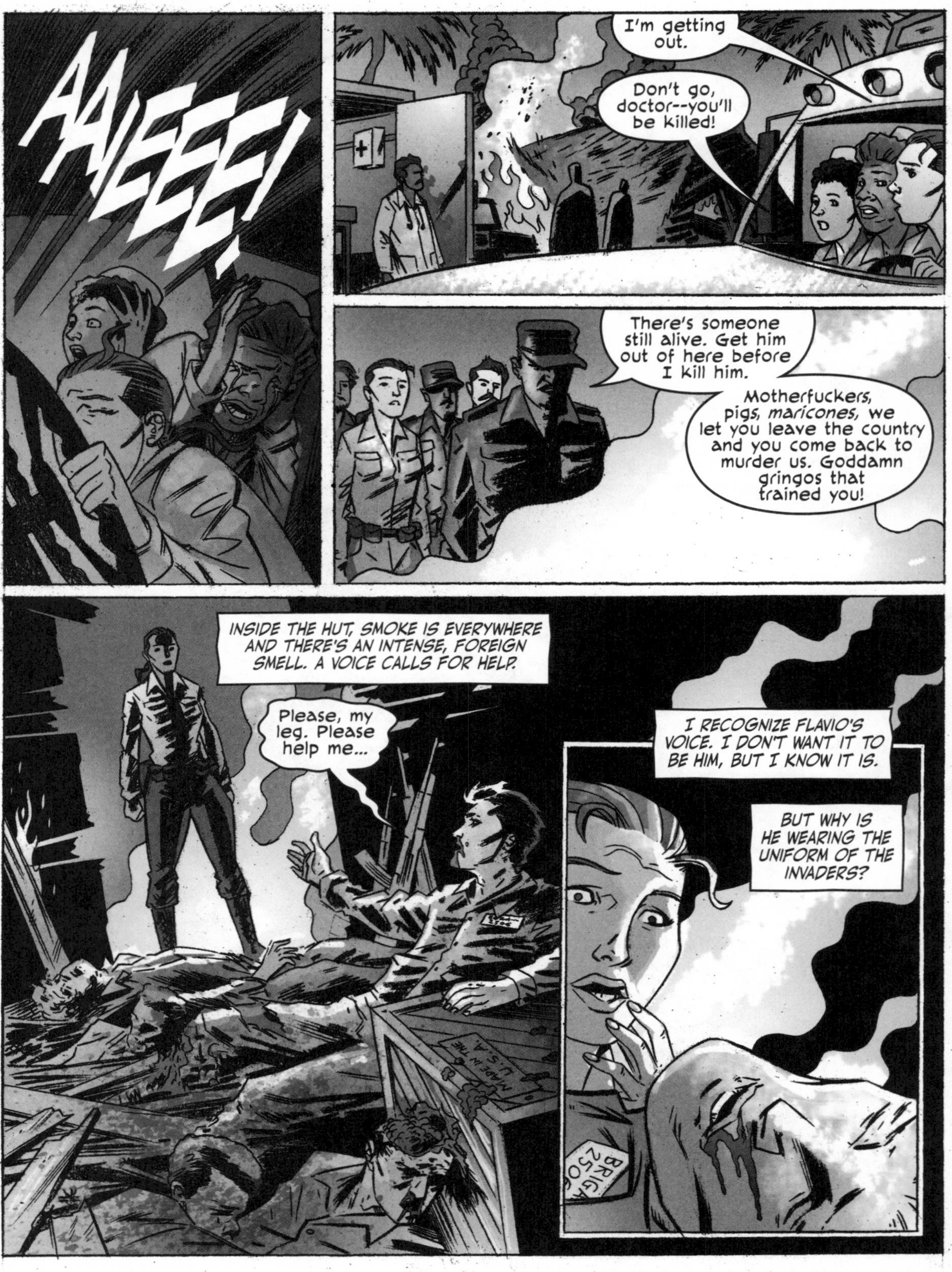
AAIEEEE!
I'm getting out.
Don't go, doctor--you'll be killed!
There's someone still alive. Get him out of here before I kill him.
Motherfuckers, pigs, *maricones*, we let you leave the country and you come back to murder us. Goddamn gringos that trained you!
INSIDE THE HUT, SMOKE IS EVERYWHERE AND THERE'S AN INTENSE, FOREIGN SMELL. A VOICE CALLS FOR HELP.
Please, my leg. Please help me...
MADE IN THE U.S.A.
I RECOGNIZE FLAVIO'S VOICE. I DON'T WANT IT TO BE HIM, BUT I KNOW IT IS.
BUT WHY IS HE WEARING THE UNIFORM OF THE INVADERS?

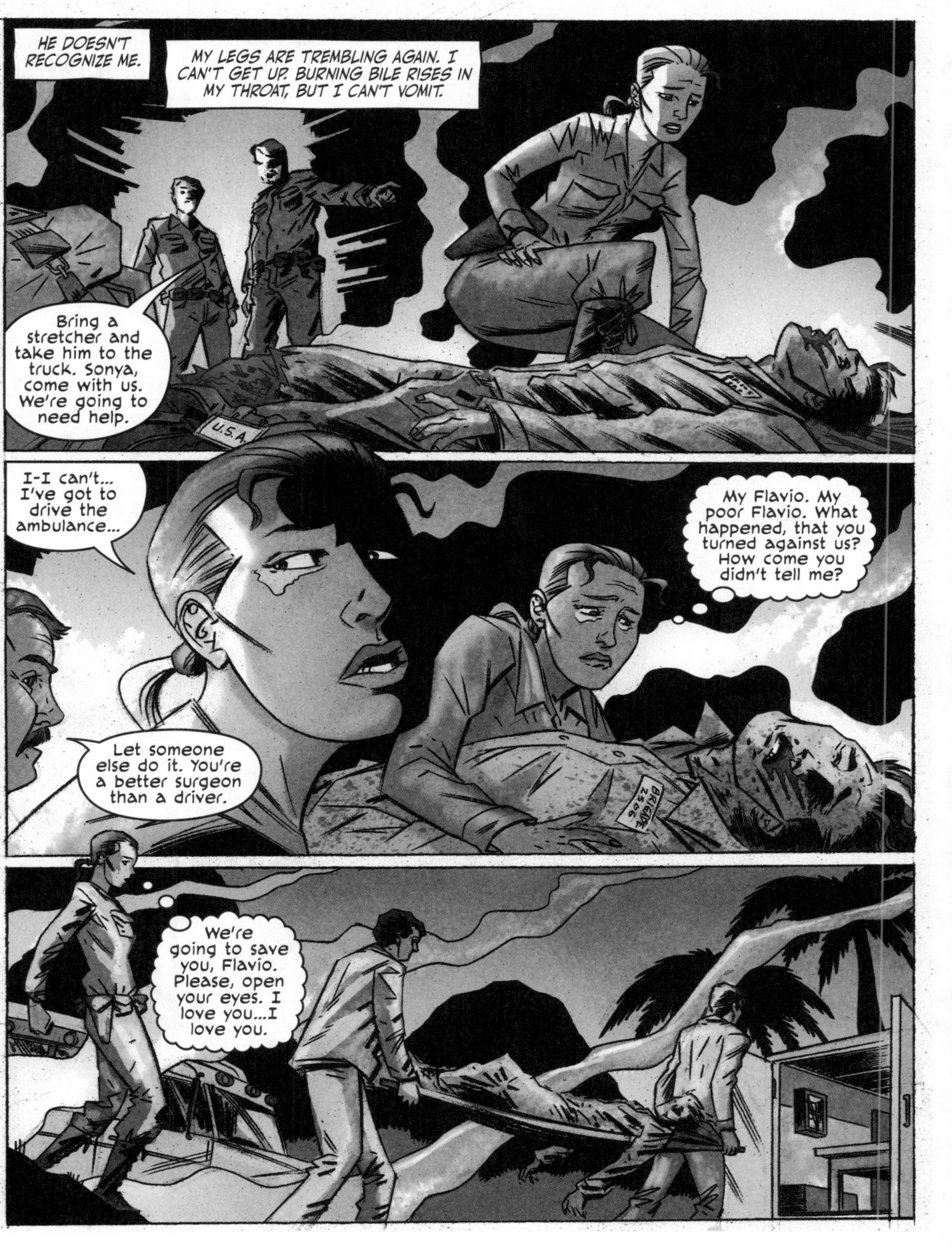

HE DOESN'T RECOGNIZE ME.
MY LEGS ARE TREMBLING AGAIN. I CAN'T GET UP. BURNING BILE RISES IN MY THROAT, BUT I CAN'T VOMIT.
Bring a stretcher and take him to the truck. Sonya, come with us. We're going to need help.
U.S.A.
I-I can't... I've got to drive the ambulance...
My Flavio. My poor Flavio. What happened, that you turned against us? How come you didn't tell me?
Let someone else do it. You're a better surgeon than a driver.
BRIGADE 2506
We're going to save you, Flavio. Please, open your eyes. I love you...I love you.

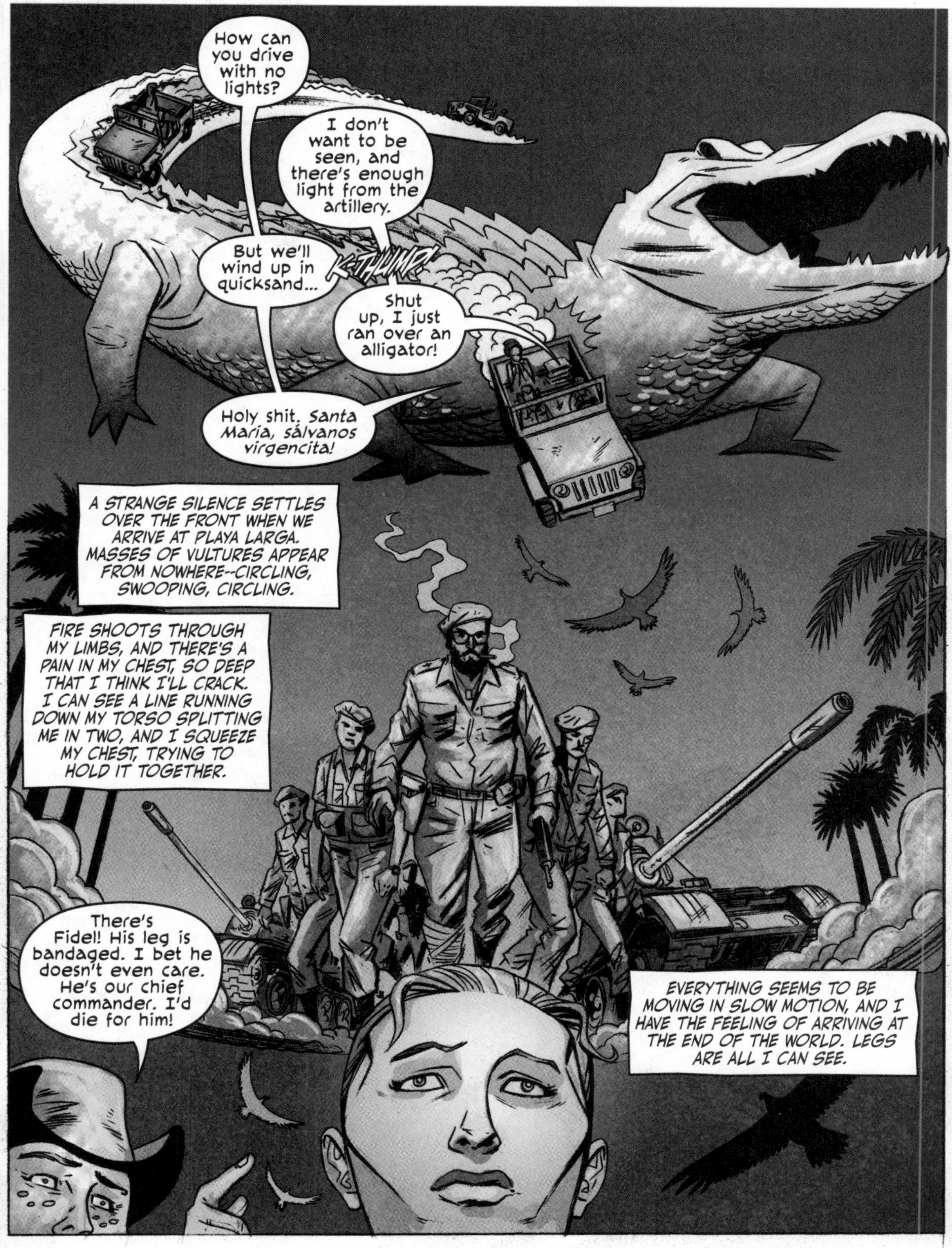
How can you drive with no lights?
I don't want to be seen, and there's enough light from the artillery.
But we'll wind up in quicksand...
K-THUMP!
Shut up, I just ran over an alligator!
Holy shit. Santa María, sálvanos virgencita!
A STRANGE SILENCE SETTLES OVER THE FRONT WHEN WE ARRIVE AT PLAYA LARGA. MASSES OF VULTURES APPEAR FROM NOWHERE--CIRCLING, SWOOPING, CIRCLING.
FIRE SHOOTS THROUGH MY LIMBS, AND THERE'S A PAIN IN MY CHEST, SO DEEP THAT I THINK I'LL CRACK. I CAN SEE A LINE RUNNING DOWN MY TORSO SPLITTING ME IN TWO, AND I SQUEEZE MY CHEST, TRYING TO HOLD IT TOGETHER.
There's Fidel! His leg is bandaged. I bet he doesn't even care. He's our chief commander. I'd die for him!
EVERYTHING SEEMS TO BE MOVING IN SLOW MOTION, AND I HAVE THE FEELING OF ARRIVING AT THE END OF THE WORLD. LEGS ARE ALL I CAN SEE.

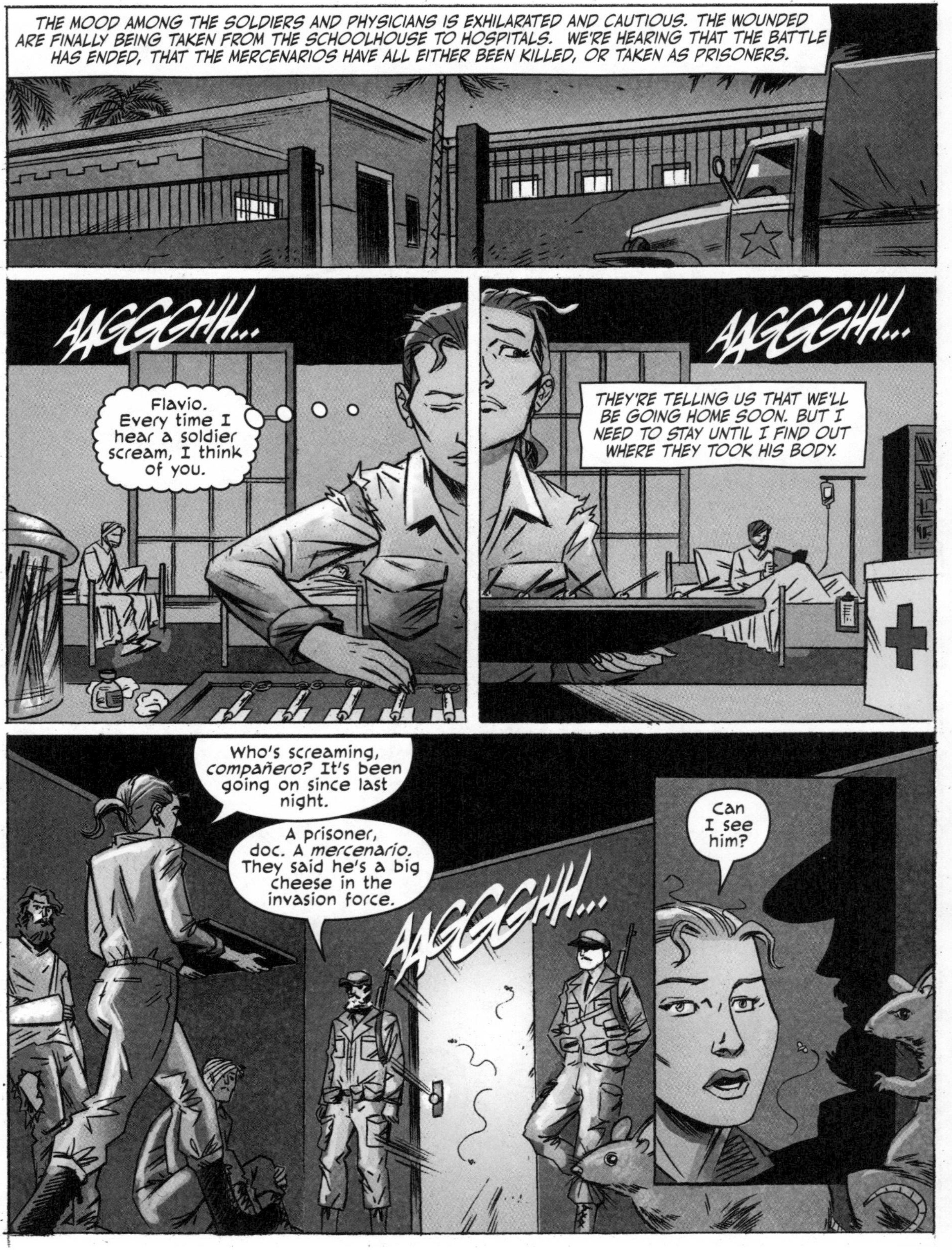
THE MOOD AMONG THE SOLDIERS AND PHYSICIANS IS EXHILARATED AND CAUTIOUS. THE WOUNDED ARE FINALLY BEING TAKEN FROM THE SCHOOLHOUSE TO HOSPITALS. WE'RE HEARING THAT THE BATTLE HAS ENDED, THAT THE MERCENARIOS HAVE ALL EITHER BEEN KILLED, OR TAKEN AS PRISONERS.
AAGGGHH...
Flavio. Every time I hear a soldier scream, I think of you.
AAGGGHH...
THEY'RE TELLING US THAT WE'LL BE GOING HOME SOON. BUT I NEED TO STAY UNTIL I FIND OUT WHERE THEY TOOK HIS BODY.
Who's screaming, *compañero?* It's been going on since last night.
A prisoner, doc. A *mercenario.* They said he's a big cheese in the invasion force.
AAGGGHH...
Can I see him?

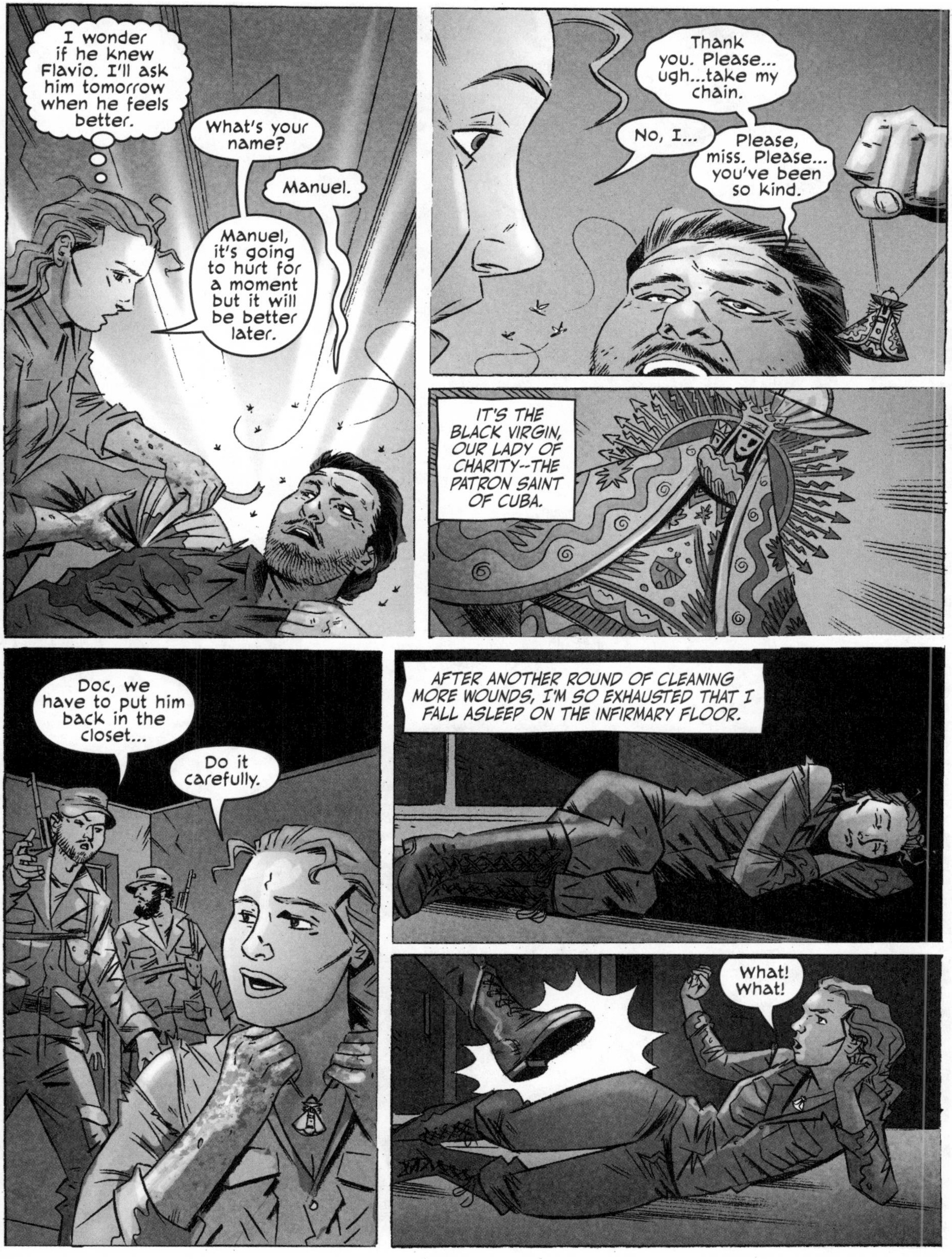
I wonder if he knew Flavio. I'll ask him tomorrow when he feels better.
What's your name?
Manuel.
Manuel, it's going to hurt for a moment but it will be better later.
Thank you. Please... ugh...take my chain.
No, I...
Please, miss. Please... you've been so kind.
IT'S THE BLACK VIRGIN, OUR LADY OF CHARITY--THE PATRON SAINT OF CUBA.
Doc, we have to put him back in the closet...
Do it carefully.
AFTER ANOTHER ROUND OF CLEANING MORE WOUNDS, I'M SO EXHAUSTED THAT I FALL ASLEEP ON THE INFIRMARY FLOOR.
What! What!

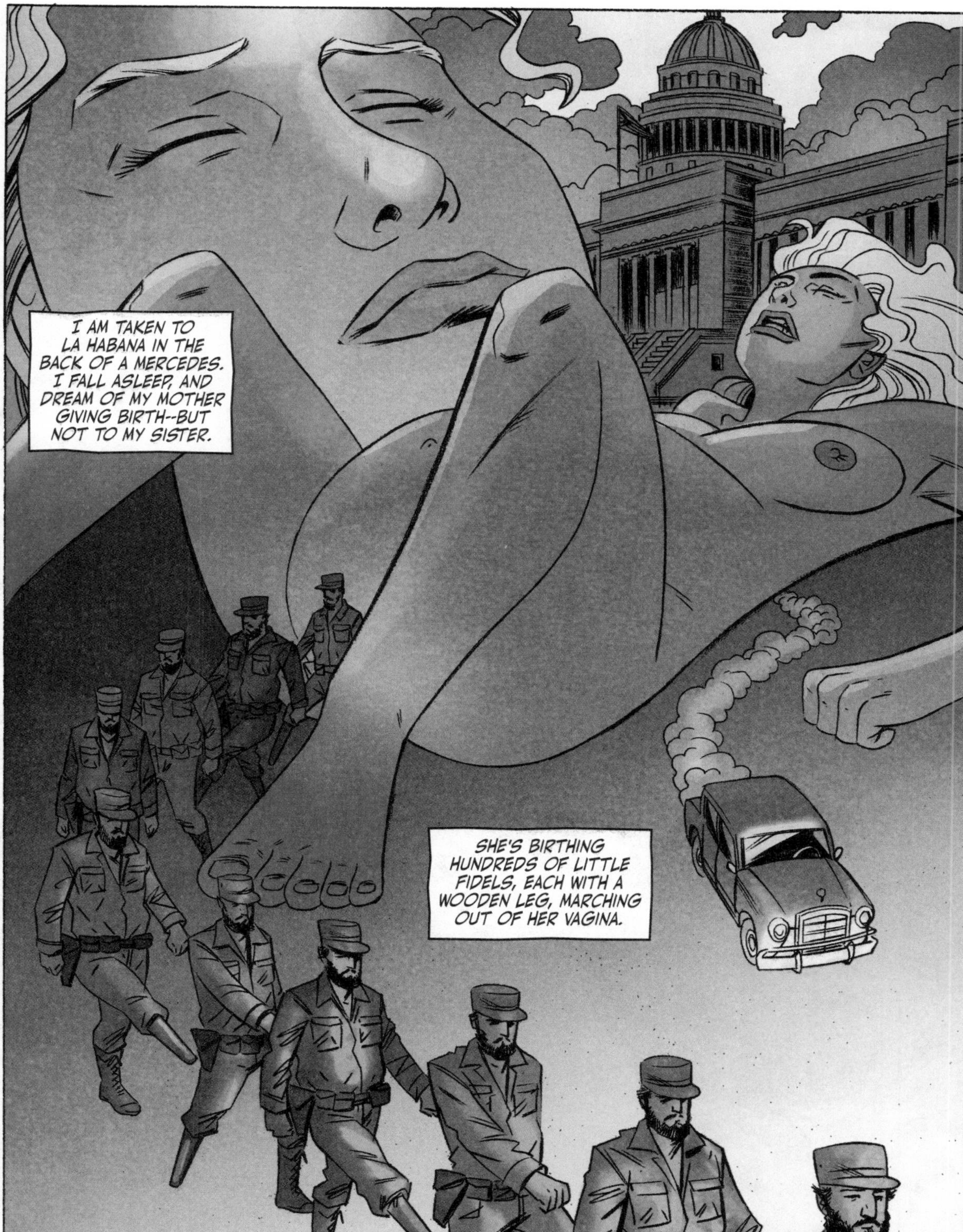
I AM TAKEN TO LA HABANA IN THE BACK OF A MERCEDES. I FALL ASLEEP, AND DREAM OF MY MOTHER GIVING BIRTH--BUT NOT TO MY SISTER.
SHE'S BIRTHING HUNDREDS OF LITTLE FIDELS, EACH WITH A WOODEN LEG, MARCHING OUT OF HER VAGINA.

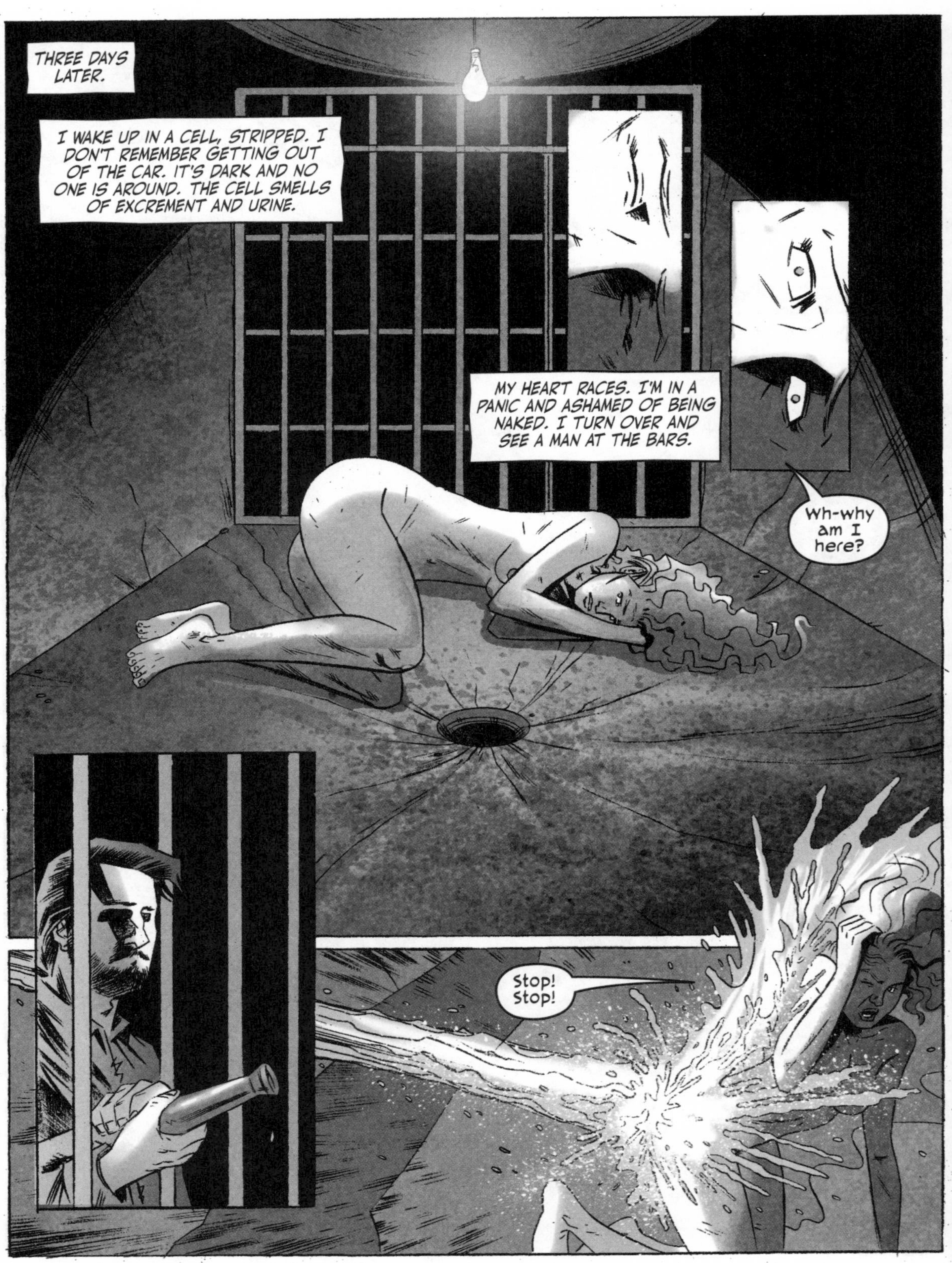
THREE DAYS LATER.
I WAKE UP IN A CELL, STRIPPED. I DON'T REMEMBER GETTING OUT OF THE CAR. IT'S DARK AND NO ONE IS AROUND. THE CELL SMELLS OF EXCREMENT AND URINE.
MY HEART RACES. I'M IN A PANIC AND ASHAMED OF BEING NAKED. I TURN OVER AND SEE A MAN AT THE BARS.
Wh-why am I here?
Stop! Stop!

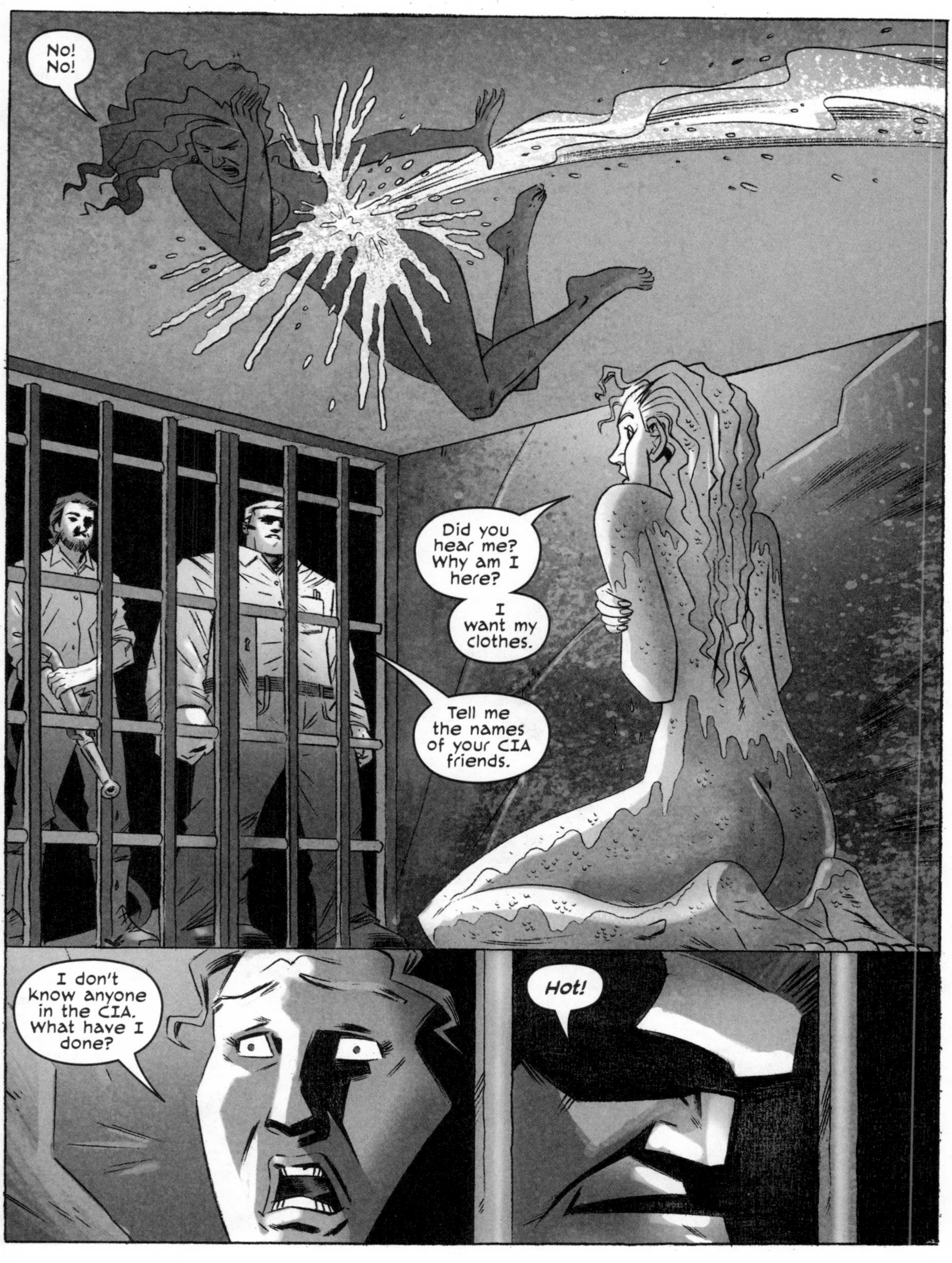
No! No!
Did you hear me? Why am I here?
I want my clothes.
Tell me the names of your CIA friends.
I don't know anyone in the CIA. What have I done?
Hot!

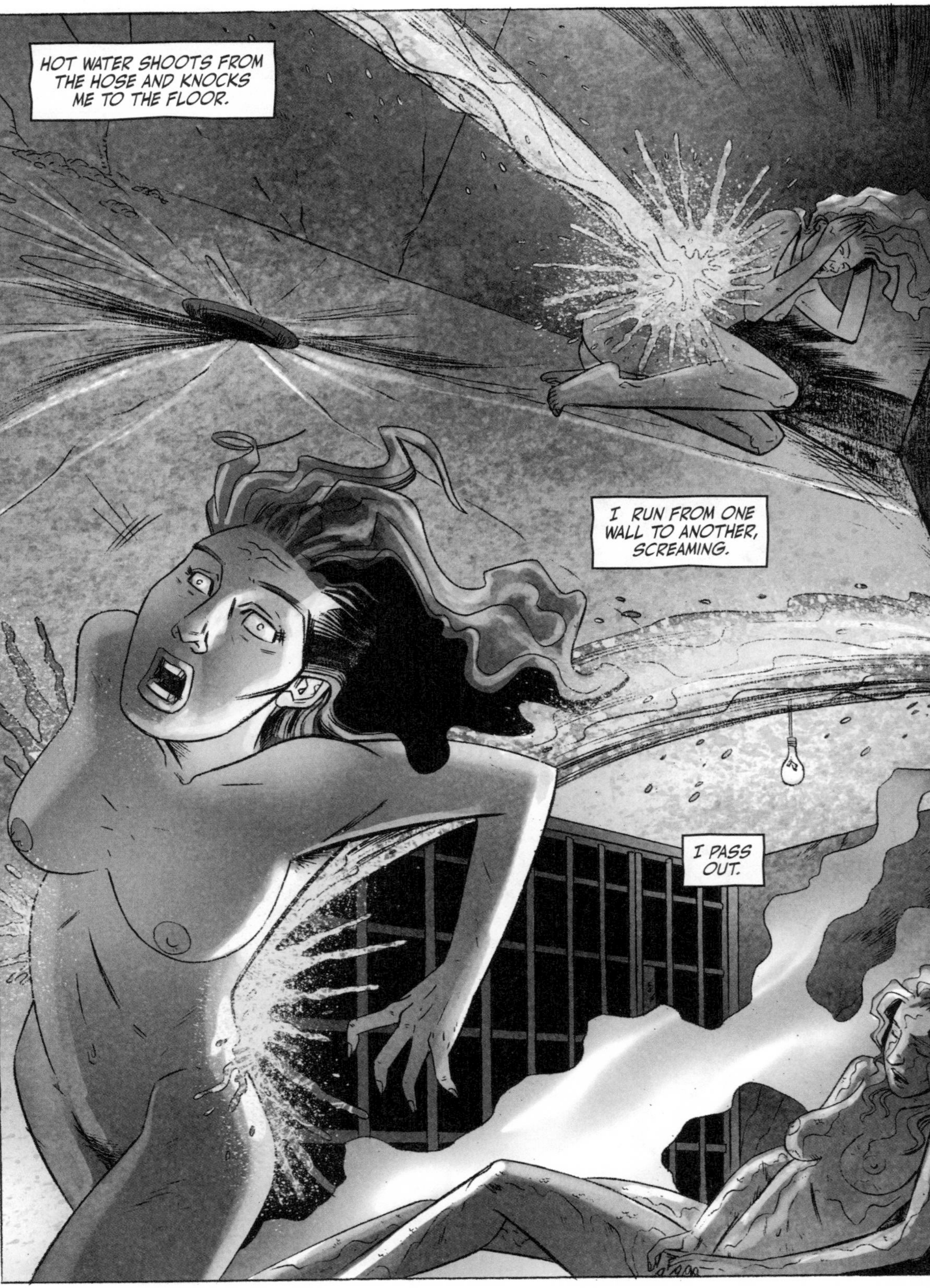
HOT WATER SHOOTS FROM THE HOSE AND KNOCKS ME TO THE FLOOR.
I RUN FROM ONE WALL TO ANOTHER, SCREAMING.
I PASS OUT.

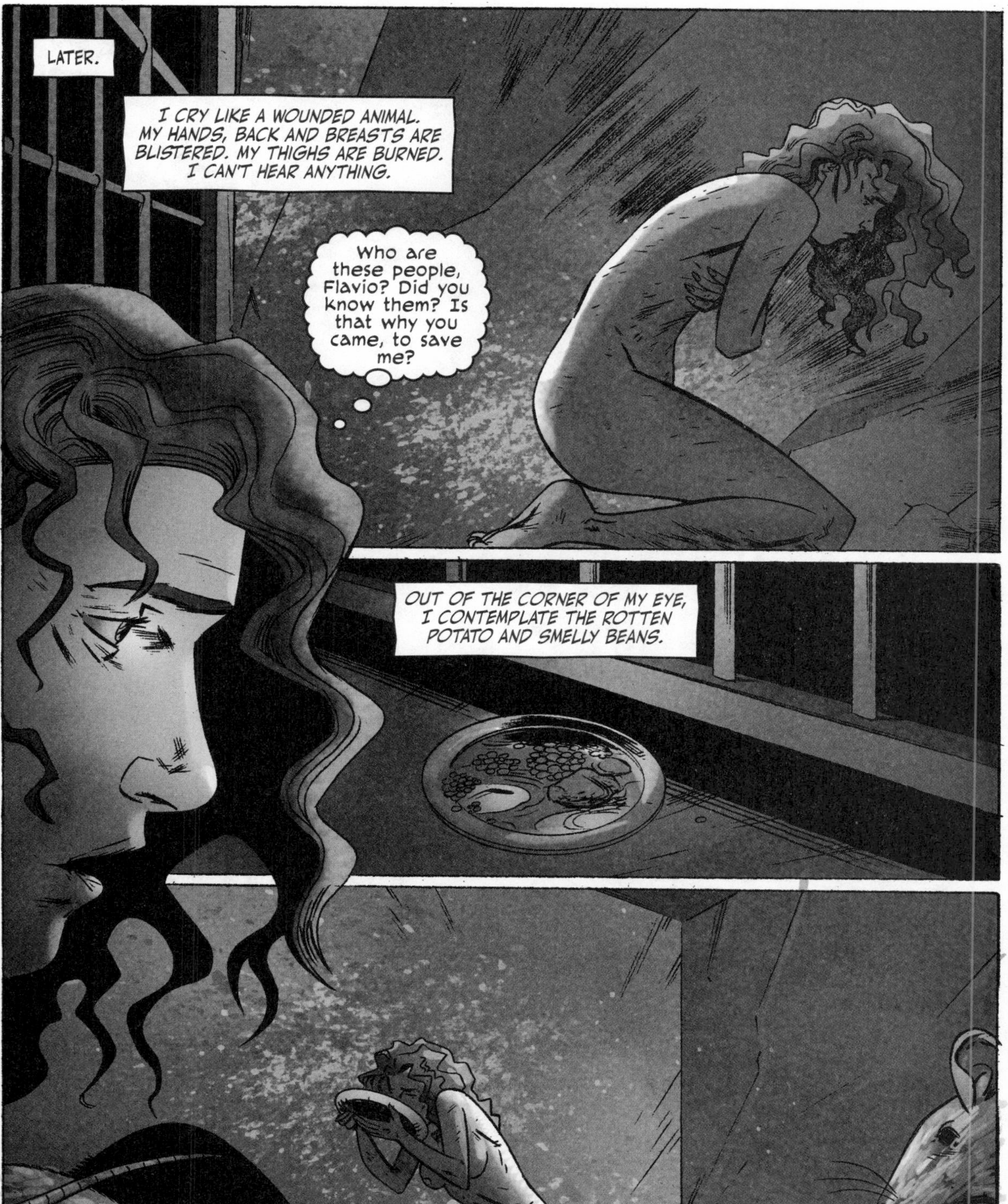
LATER.
I CRY LIKE A WOUNDED ANIMAL. MY HANDS, BACK AND BREASTS ARE BLISTERED. MY THIGHS ARE BURNED. I CAN'T HEAR ANYTHING.
Who are these people, Flavio? Did you know them? Is that why you came, to save me?
OUT OF THE CORNER OF MY EYE, I CONTEMPLATE THE ROTTEN POTATO AND SMELLY BEANS.

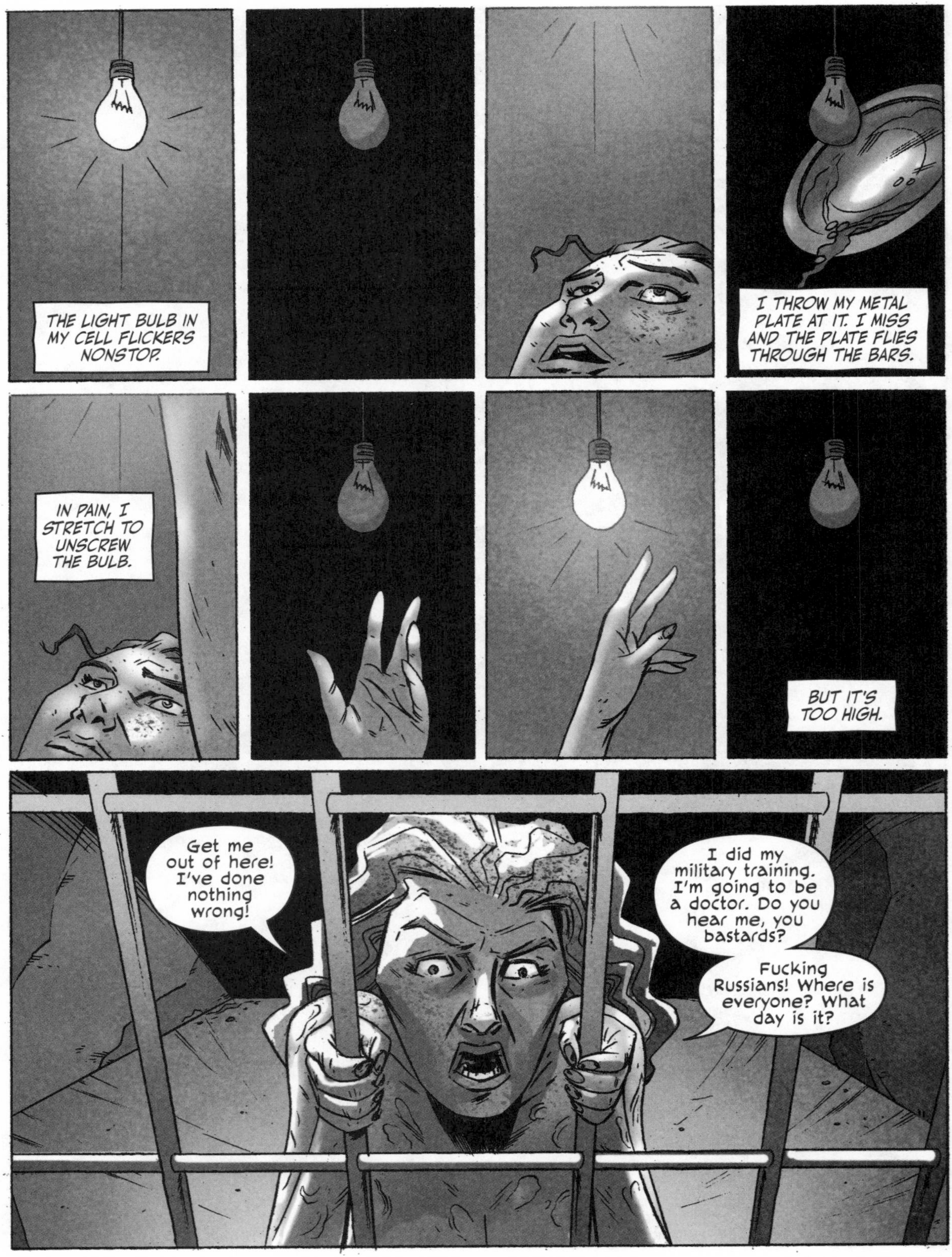
THE LIGHT BULB IN MY CELL FLICKERS NONSTOP.
I THROW MY METAL PLATE AT IT. I MISS AND THE PLATE FLIES THROUGH THE BARS.
IN PAIN, I STRETCH TO UNSCREW THE BULB.
BUT IT'S TOO HIGH.
Get me out of here! I've done nothing wrong!
I did my military training. I'm going to be a doctor. Do you hear me, you bastards?
Fucking Russians! Where is everyone? What day is it?

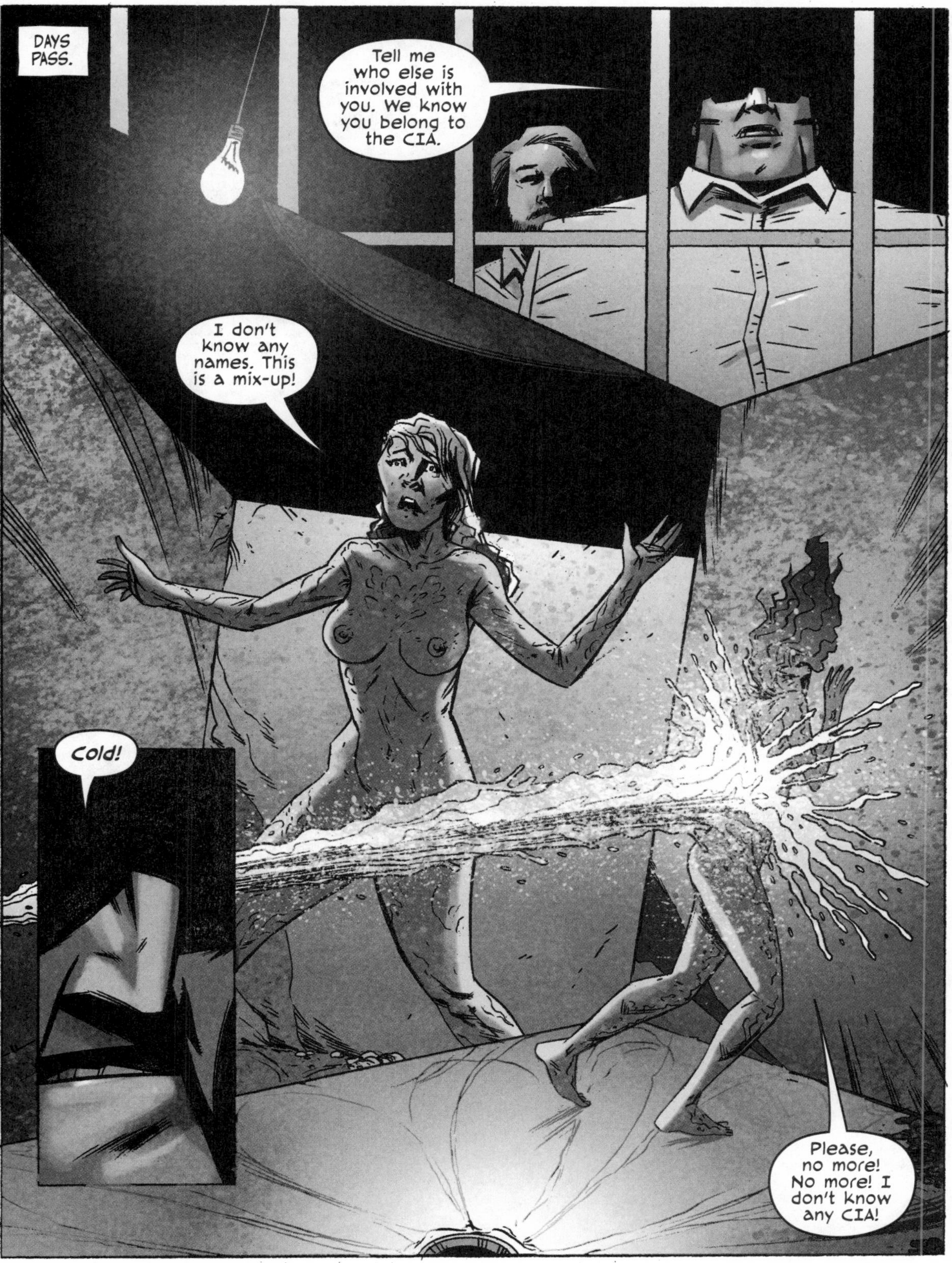
DAYS PASS.
Tell me who else is involved with you. We know you belong to the CIA.
I don't know any names. This is a mix-up!
Cold!
Please, no more! No more! I don't know any CIA!

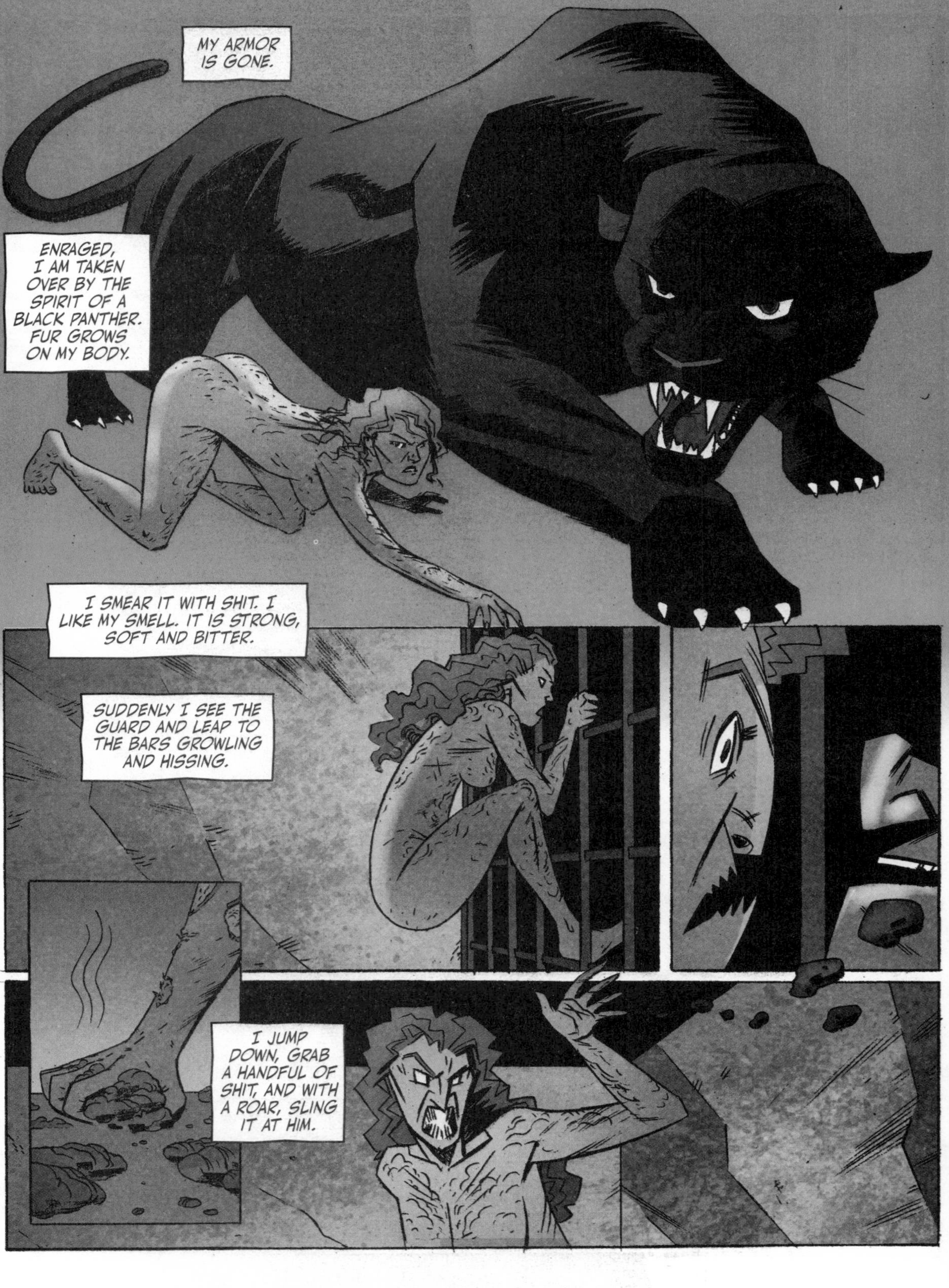
MY ARMOR IS GONE.
ENRAGED, I AM TAKEN OVER BY THE SPIRIT OF A BLACK PANTHER. FUR GROWS ON MY BODY.
I SMEAR IT WITH SHIT. I LIKE MY SMELL. IT IS STRONG, SOFT AND BITTER.
SUDDENLY I SEE THE GUARD AND LEAP TO THE BARS GROWLING AND HISSING.
I JUMP DOWN, GRAB A HANDFUL OF SHIT, AND WITH A ROAR, SLING IT AT HIM.

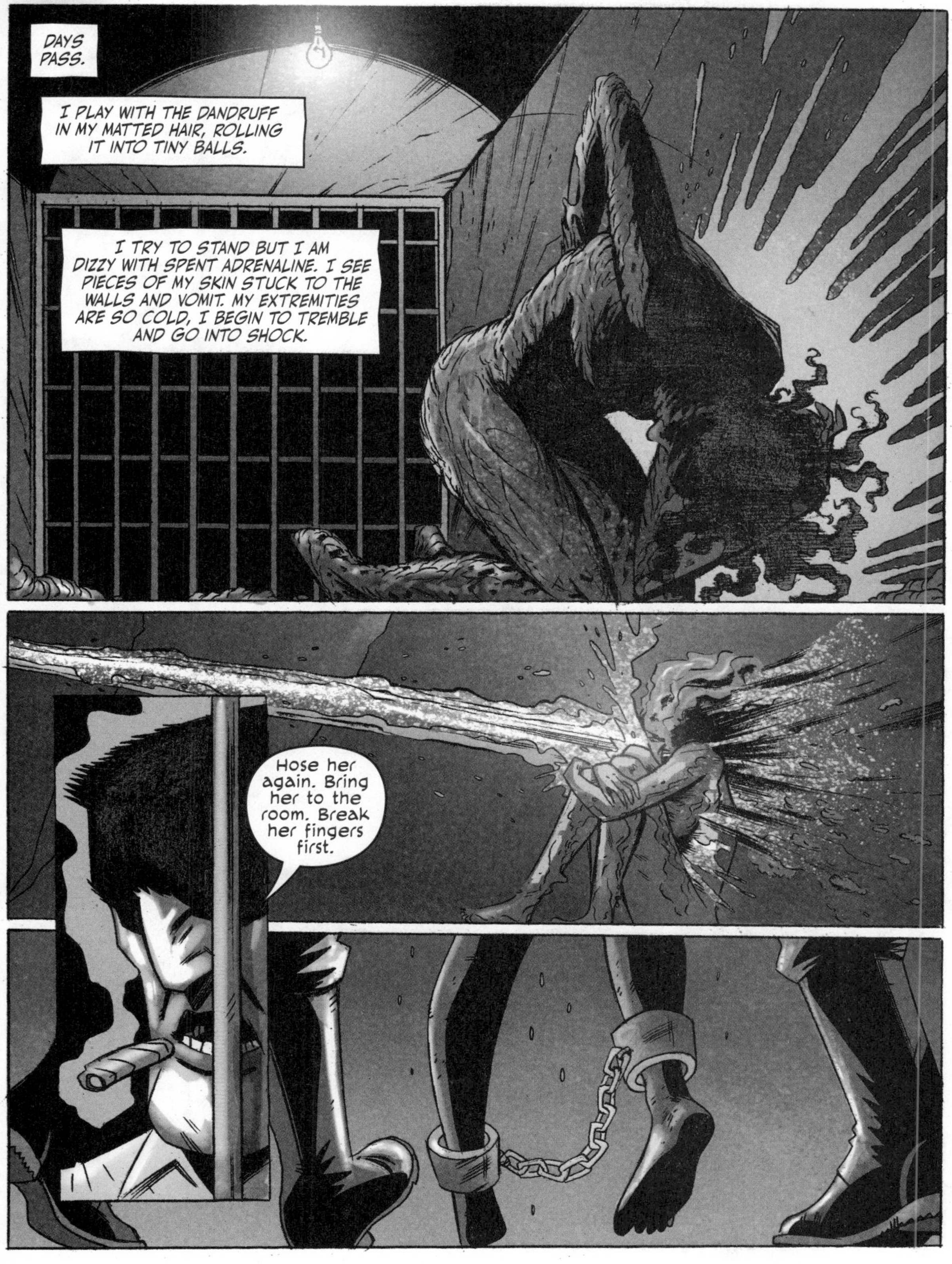
DAYS PASS.
I PLAY WITH THE DANDRUFF IN MY MATTED HAIR, ROLLING IT INTO TINY BALLS.
I TRY TO STAND BUT I AM DIZZY WITH SPENT ADRENALINE. I SEE PIECES OF MY SKIN STUCK TO THE WALLS AND VOMIT. MY EXTREMITIES ARE SO COLD, I BEGIN TO TREMBLE AND GO INTO SHOCK.
Hose her again. Bring her to the room. Break her fingers first.

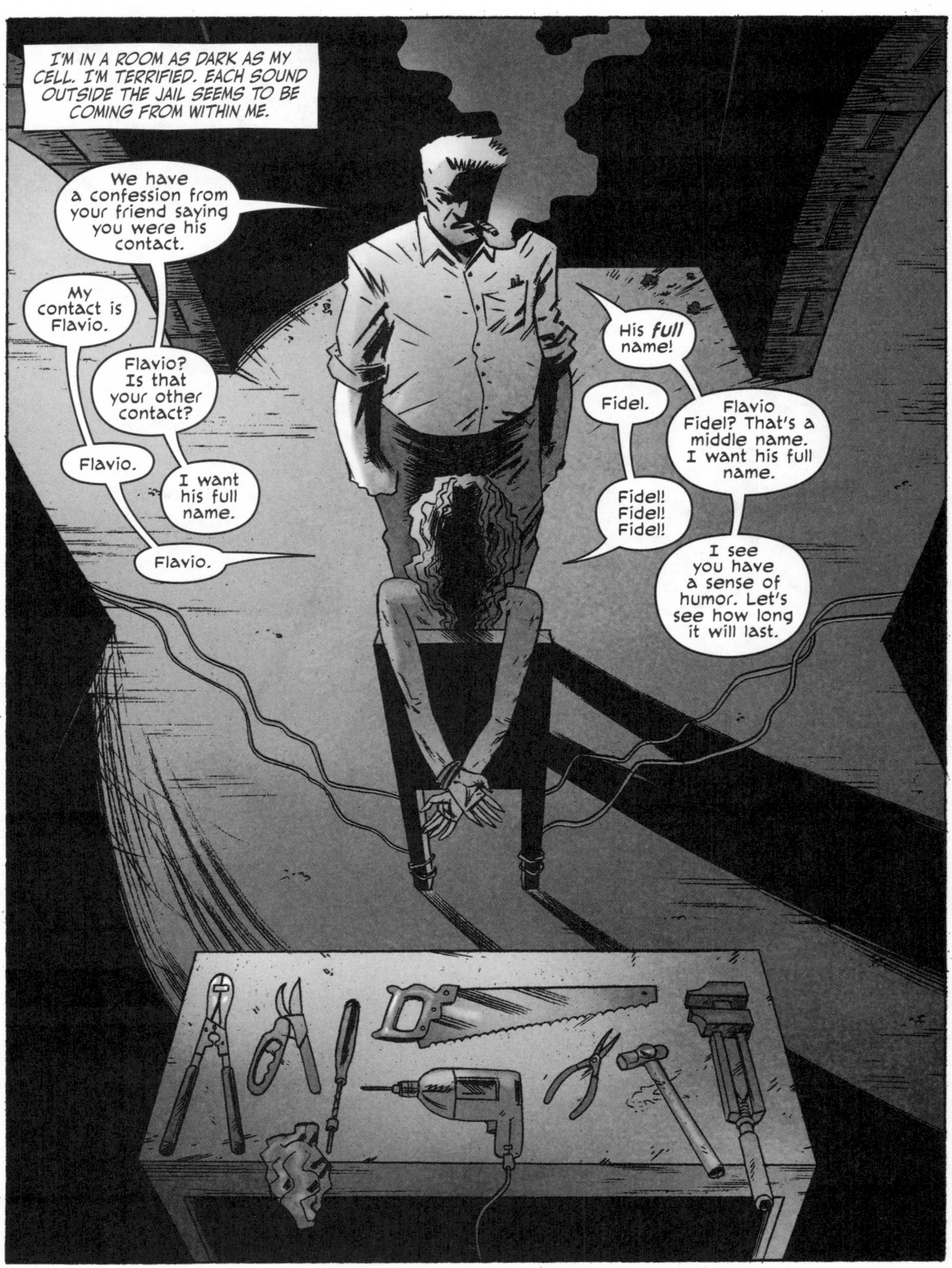
I'M IN A ROOM AS DARK AS MY CELL. I'M TERRIFIED. EACH SOUND OUTSIDE THE JAIL SEEMS TO BE COMING FROM WITHIN ME.
We have a confession from your friend saying you were his contact.
My contact is Flavio.
Flavio? Is that your other contact?
Flavio.
I want his full name.
Flavio.
His *full* name!
Fidel.
Flavio Fidel? That's a middle name. I want his full name.
Fidel! Fidel! Fidel!
I see you have a sense of humor. Let's see how long it will last.

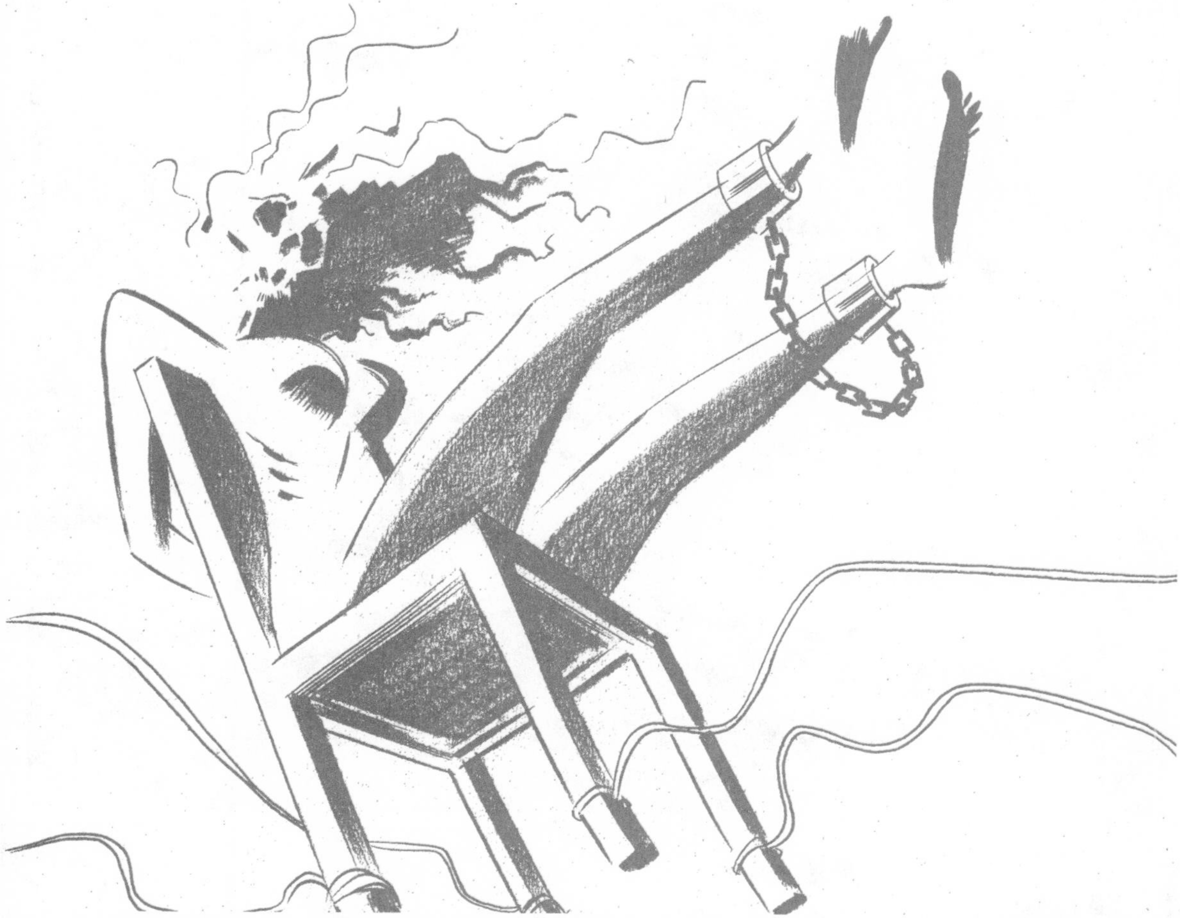

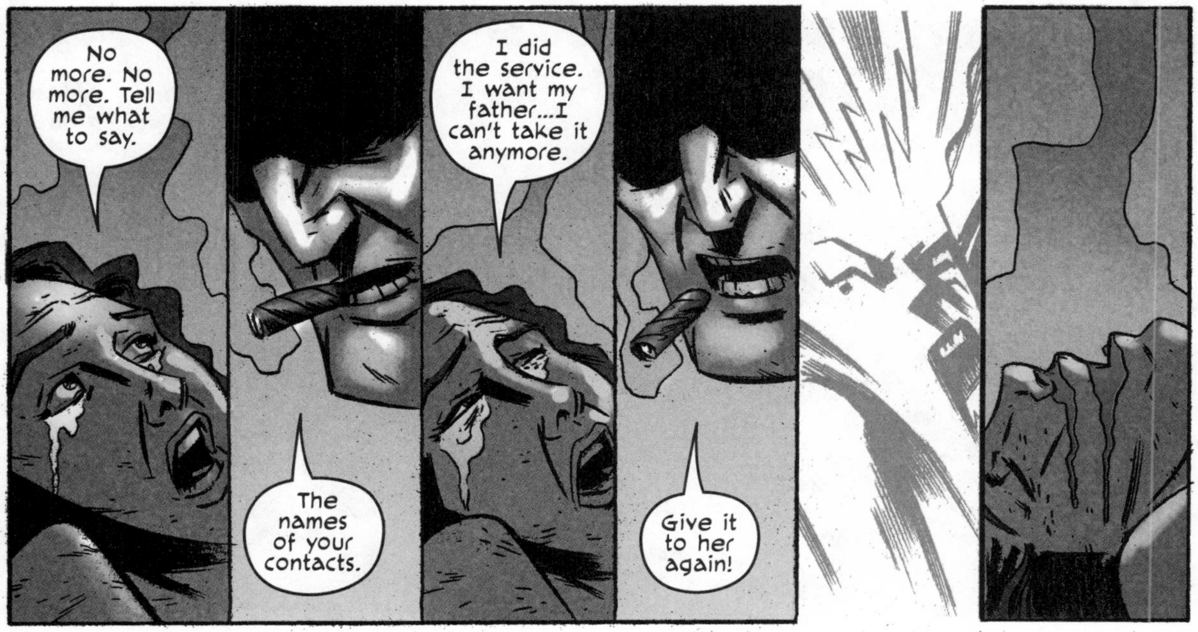
No more. No more. Tell me what to say.
The names of your contacts.
I did the service. I want my father...I can't take it anymore.
Give it to her again!

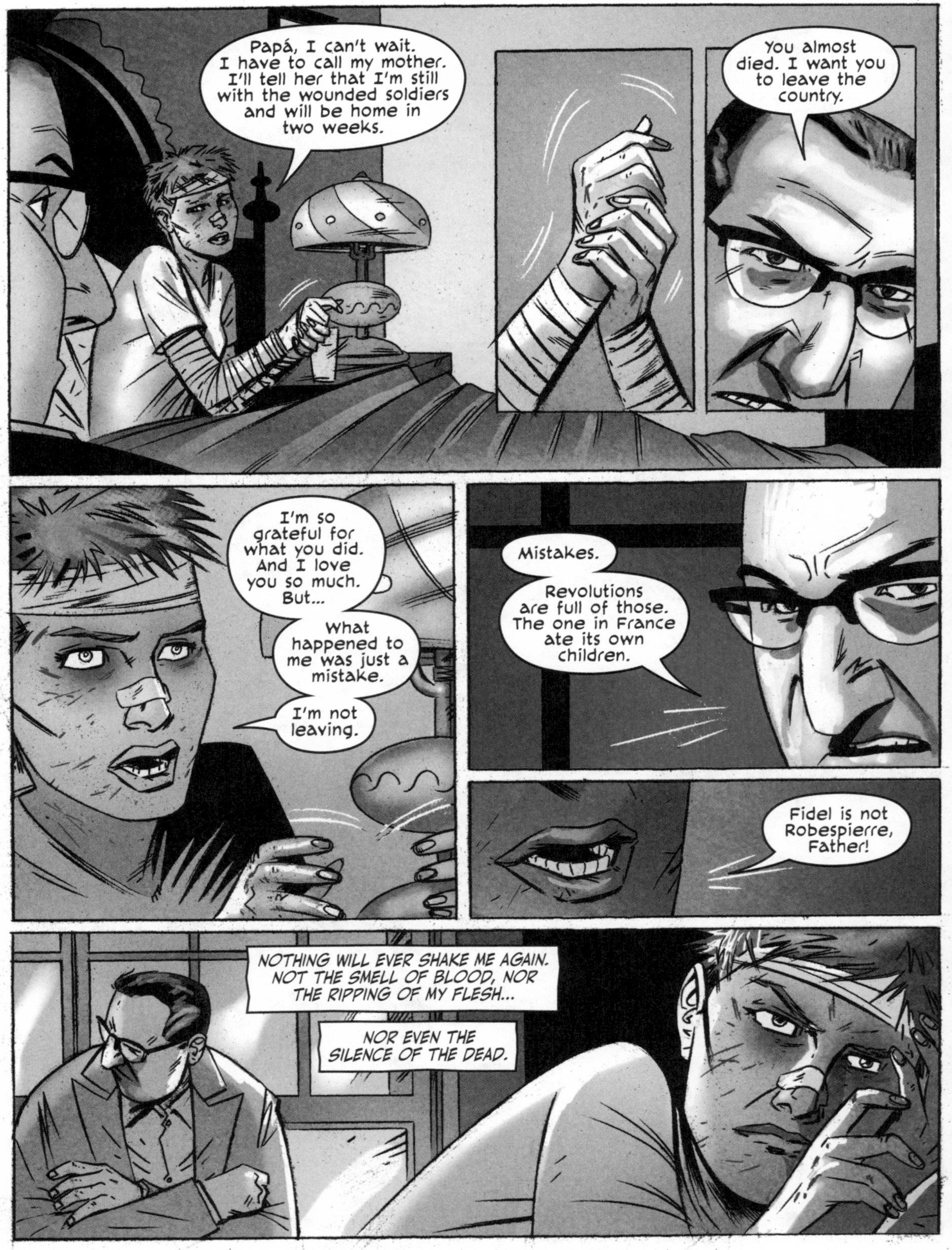
Papá, I can't wait. I have to call my mother. I'll tell her that I'm still with the wounded soldiers and will be home in two weeks.
You almost died. I want you to leave the country.
I'm so grateful for what you did. And I love you so much. But...
What happened to me was just a mistake.
I'm not leaving.
Mistakes.
Revolutions are full of those. The one in France ate its own children.
Fidel is not Robespierre, Father!
NOTHING WILL EVER SHAKE ME AGAIN. NOT THE SMELL OF BLOOD, NOR THE RIPPING OF MY FLESH...
NOR EVEN THE SILENCE OF THE DEAD.

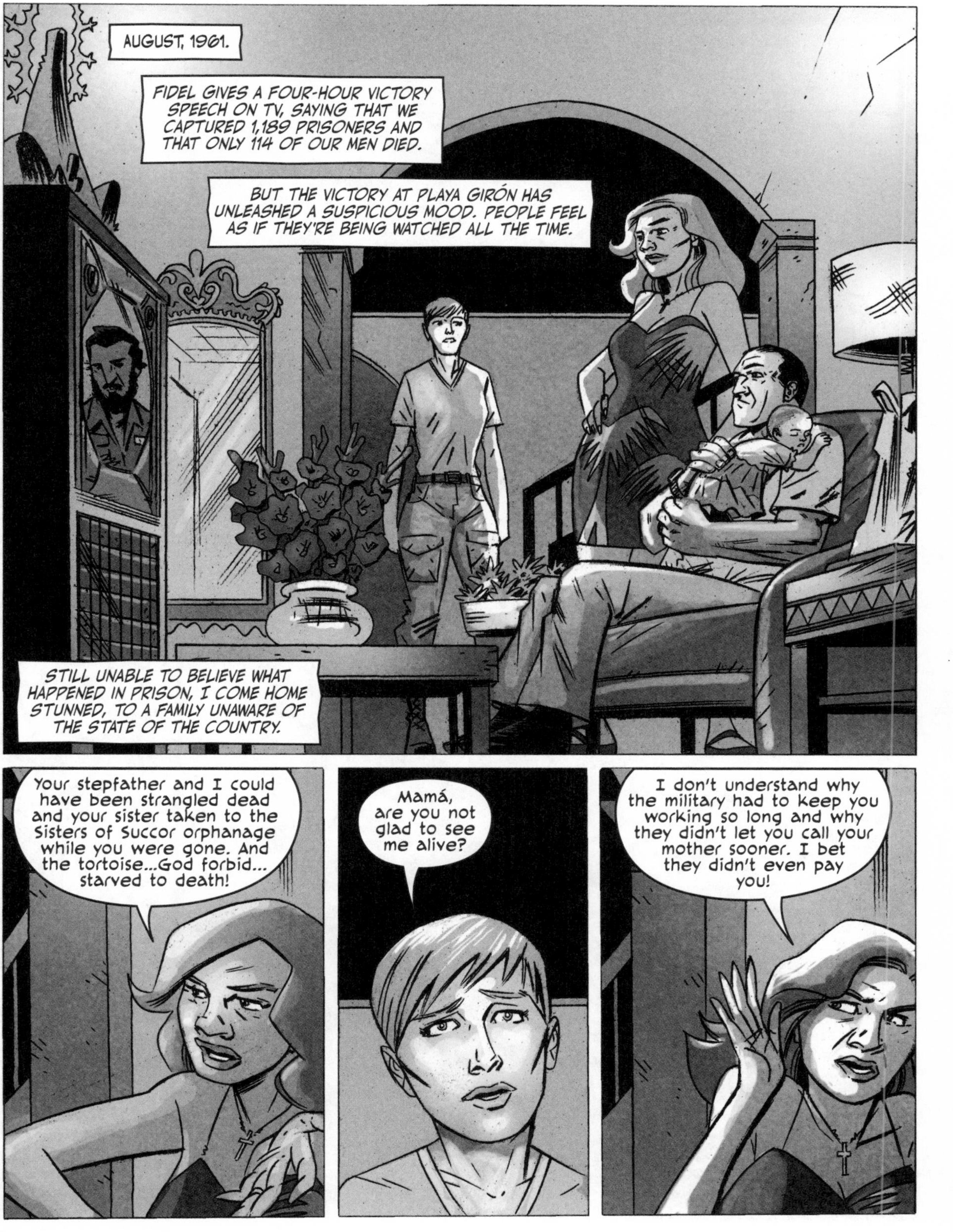
AUGUST, 1961.
FIDEL GIVES A FOUR-HOUR VICTORY SPEECH ON TV, SAYING THAT WE CAPTURED 1,189 PRISONERS AND THAT ONLY 114 OF OUR MEN DIED.
BUT THE VICTORY AT PLAYA GIRÓN HAS UNLEASHED A SUSPICIOUS MOOD. PEOPLE FEEL AS IF THEY'RE BEING WATCHED ALL THE TIME.
STILL UNABLE TO BELIEVE WHAT HAPPENED IN PRISON, I COME HOME STUNNED, TO A FAMILY UNAWARE OF THE STATE OF THE COUNTRY.
Your stepfather and I could have been strangled dead and your sister taken to the Sisters of Succor orphanage while you were gone. And the tortoise...God forbid... starved to death!
Mamá, are you not glad to see me alive?
I don't understand why the military had to keep you working so long and why they didn't let you call your mother sooner. I bet they didn't even pay you!

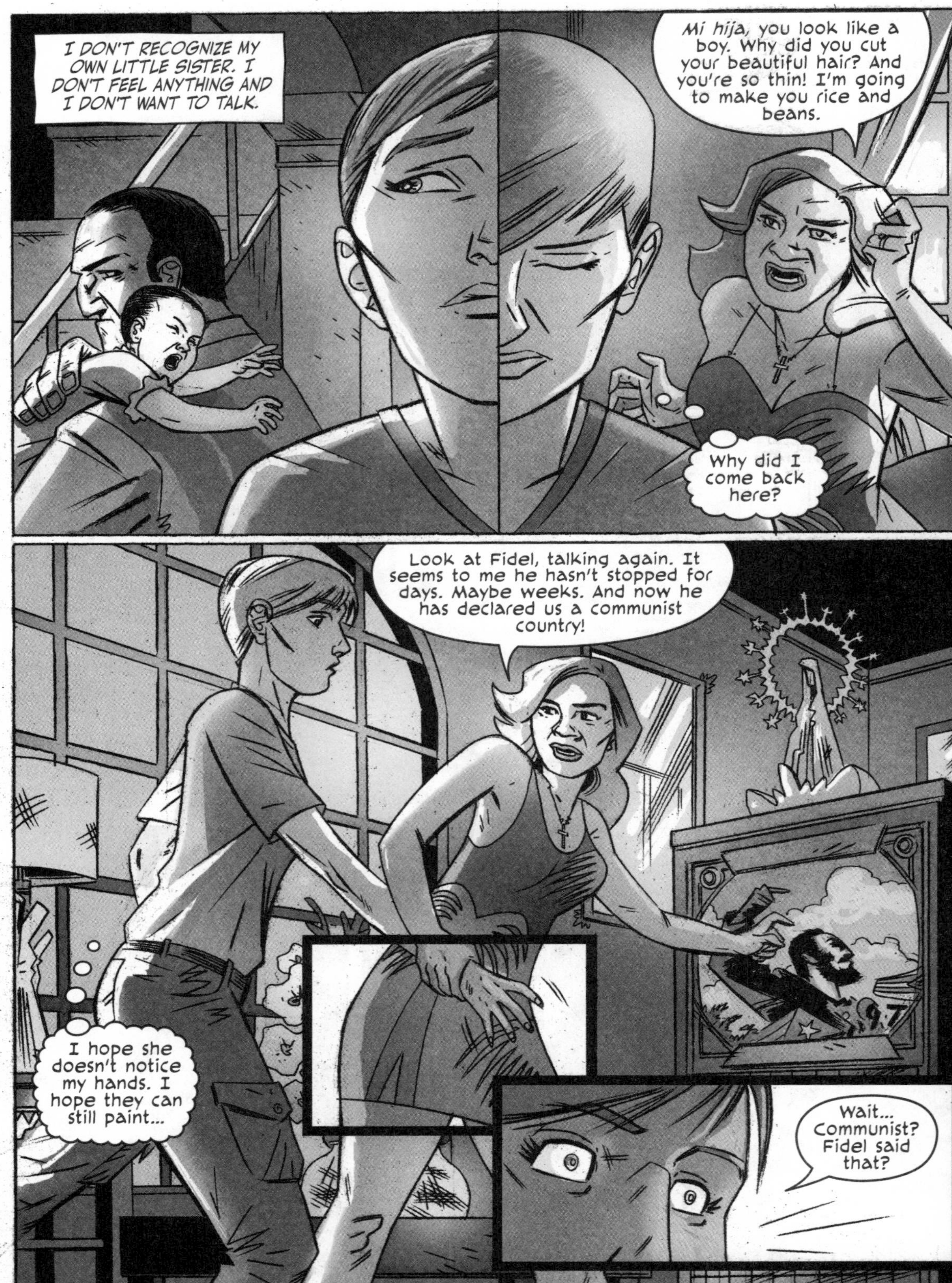
I DON'T RECOGNIZE MY OWN LITTLE SISTER. I DON'T FEEL ANYTHING AND I DON'T WANT TO TALK.
Mi hija, you look like a boy. Why did you cut your beautiful hair? And you're so thin! I'm going to make you rice and beans.
Why did I come back here?
Look at Fidel, talking again. It seems to me he hasn't stopped for days. Maybe weeks. And now he has declared us a communist country!
I hope she doesn't notice my hands. I hope they can still paint...
Wait... Communist? Fidel said that?

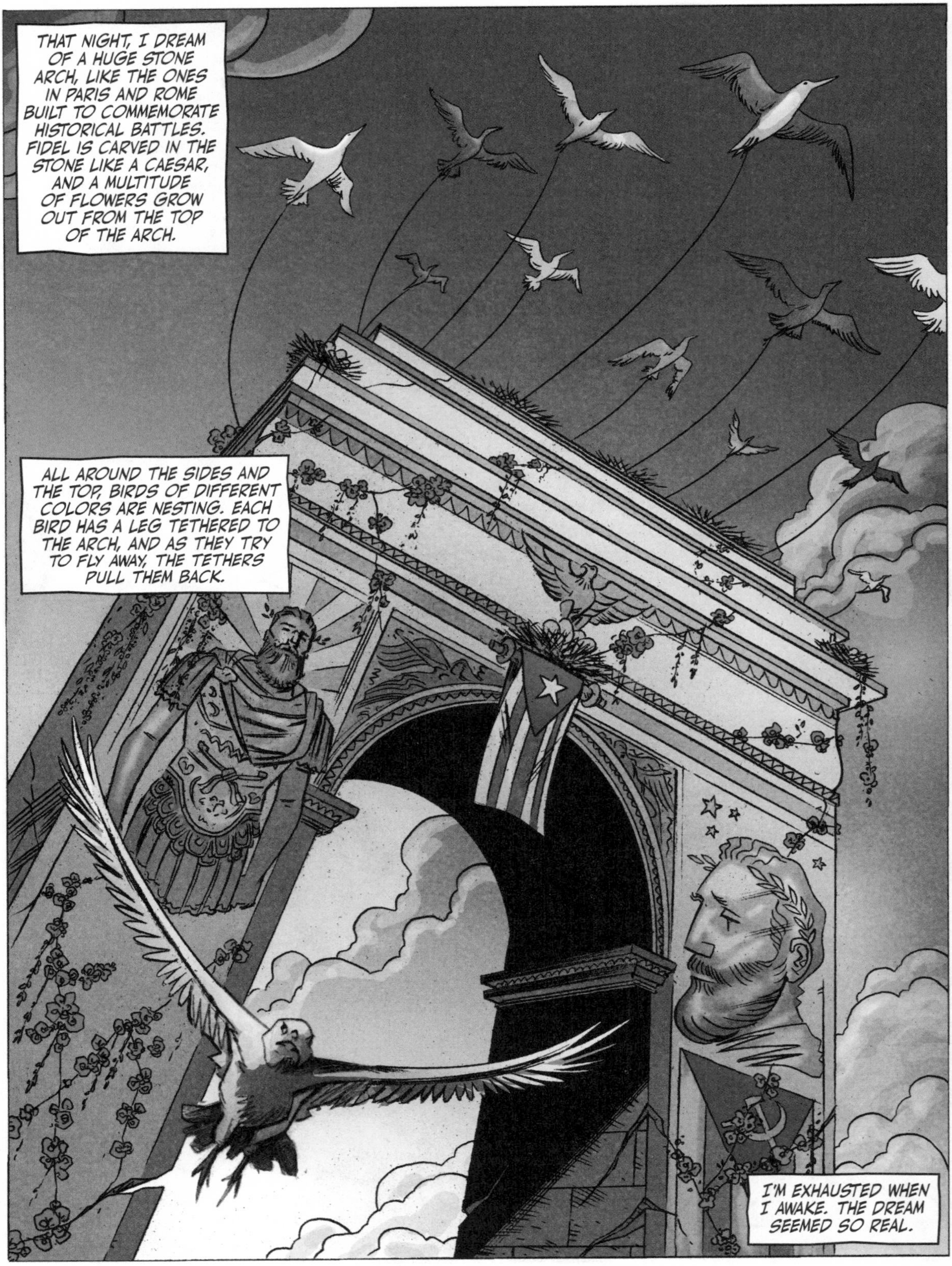
THAT NIGHT, I DREAM OF A HUGE STONE ARCH, LIKE THE ONES IN PARIS AND ROME BUILT TO COMMEMORATE HISTORICAL BATTLES. FIDEL IS CARVED IN THE STONE LIKE A CAESAR, AND A MULTITUDE OF FLOWERS GROW OUT FROM THE TOP OF THE ARCH.
ALL AROUND THE SIDES AND THE TOP, BIRDS OF DIFFERENT COLORS ARE NESTING. EACH BIRD HAS A LEG TETHERED TO THE ARCH, AND AS THEY TRY TO FLY AWAY, THE TETHERS PULL THEM BACK.
I'M EXHAUSTED WHEN I AWAKE. THE DREAM SEEMED SO REAL.

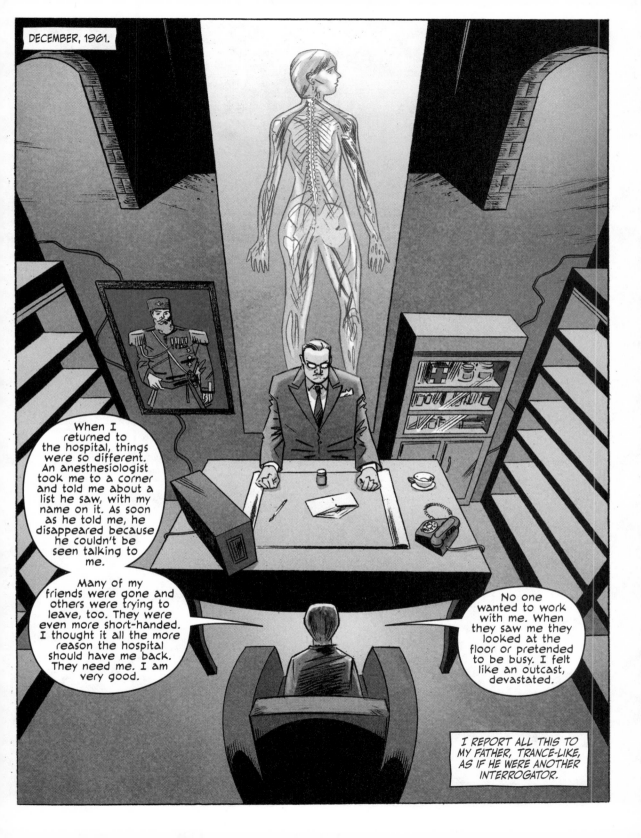

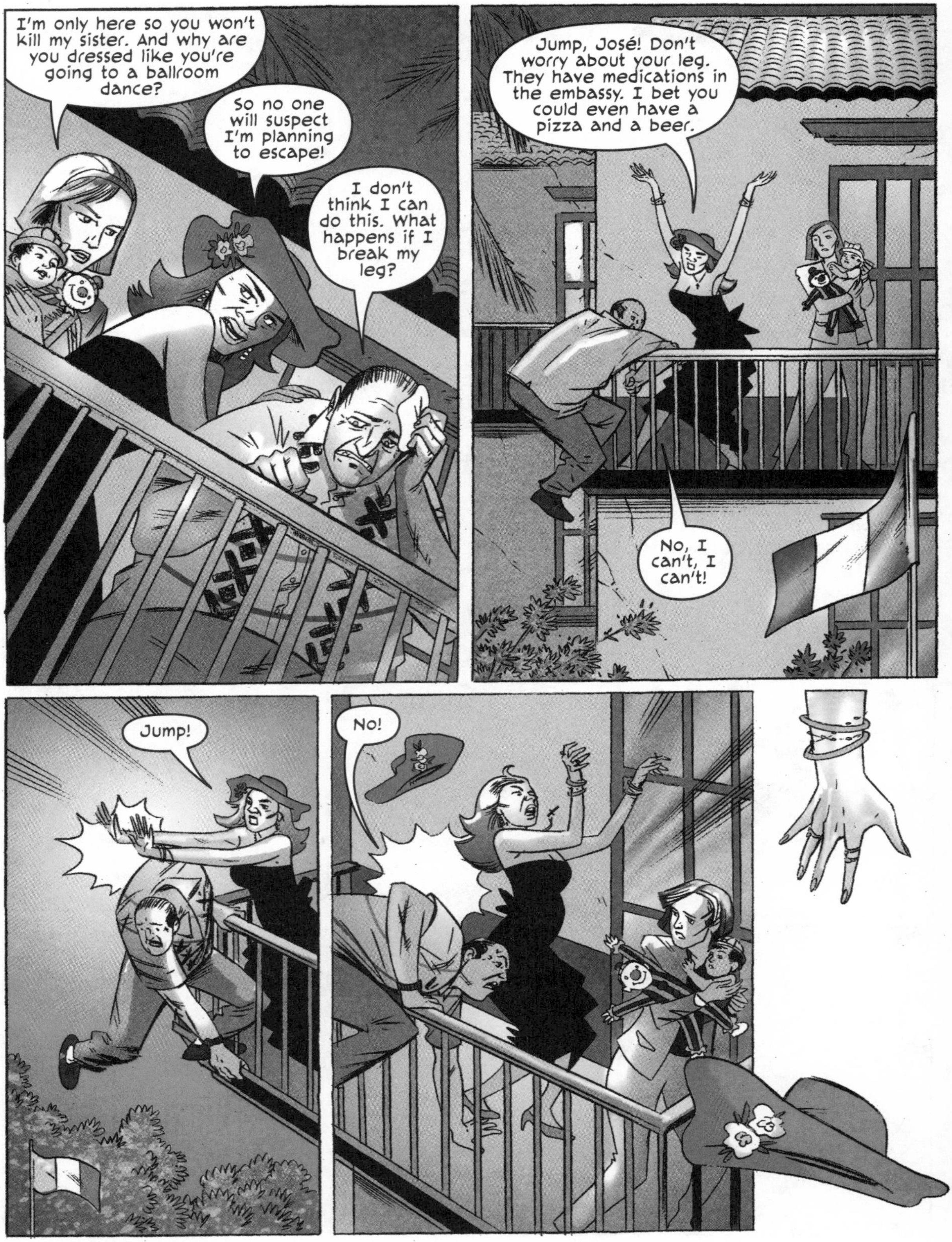
I'm only here so you won't kill my sister. And why are you dressed like you're going to a ballroom dance?
So no one will suspect I'm planning to escape!
I don't think I can do this. What happens if I break my leg?
Jump, José! Don't worry about your leg. They have medications in the embassy. I bet you could even have a pizza and a beer.
No, I can't, I can't!
Jump!
No!

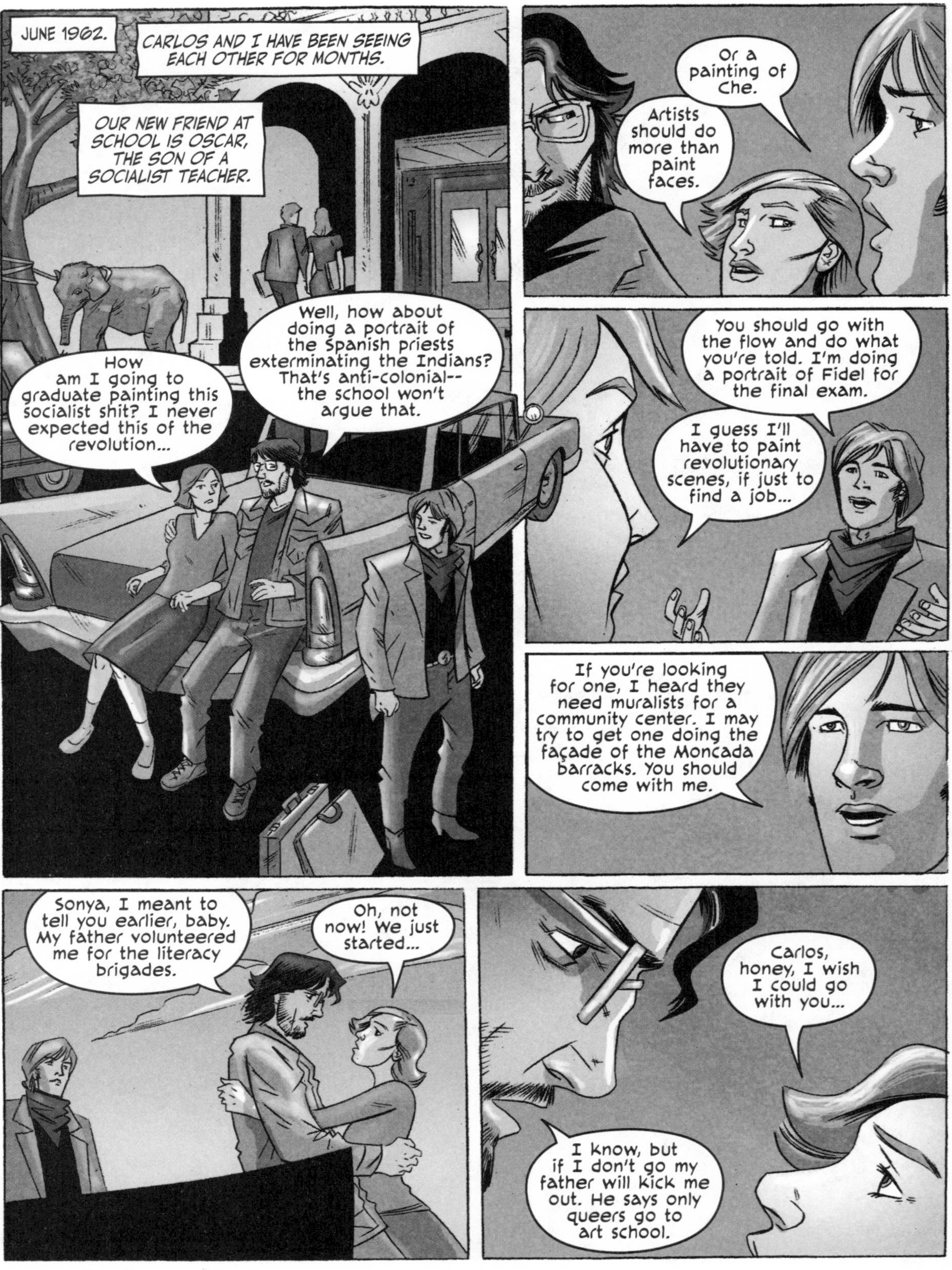
JUNE 1962.
CARLOS AND I HAVE BEEN SEEING EACH OTHER FOR MONTHS.
OUR NEW FRIEND AT SCHOOL IS OSCAR, THE SON OF A SOCIALIST TEACHER.
How am I going to graduate painting this socialist shit? I never expected this of the revolution...
Well, how about doing a portrait of the Spanish priests exterminating the Indians? That's anti-colonial-- the school won't argue that.
Or a painting of Che.
Artists should do more than paint faces.
You should go with the flow and do what you're told. I'm doing a portrait of Fidel for the final exam.
I guess I'll have to paint revolutionary scenes, if just to find a job...
If you're looking for one, I heard they need muralists for a community center. I may try to get one doing the façade of the Moncada barracks. You should come with me.
Sonya, I meant to tell you earlier, baby. My father volunteered me for the literacy brigades.
Oh, not now! We just started...
Carlos, honey, I wish I could go with you...
I know, but if I don't go my father will kick me out. He says only queers go to art school.

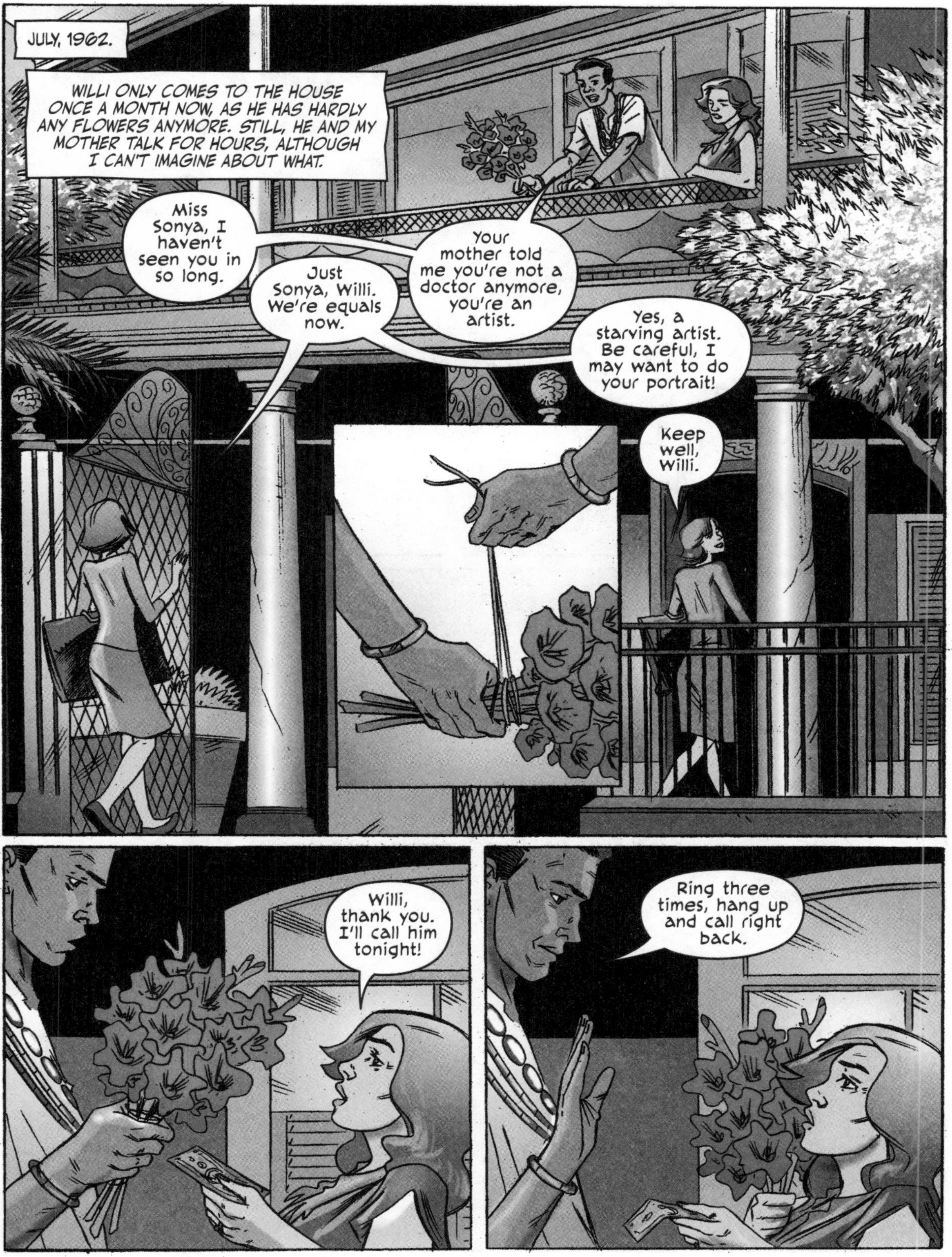
JULY, 1962.
WILLI ONLY COMES TO THE HOUSE ONCE A MONTH NOW, AS HE HAS HARDLY ANY FLOWERS ANYMORE. STILL, HE AND MY MOTHER TALK FOR HOURS, ALTHOUGH I CAN'T IMAGINE ABOUT WHAT.
Miss Sonya, I haven't seen you in so long.
Your mother told me you're not a doctor anymore, you're an artist.
Just Sonya, Willi. We're equals now.
Yes, a starving artist. Be careful, I may want to do your portrait!
Keep well, Willi.
Willi, thank you. I'll call him tonight!
Ring three times, hang up and call right back.

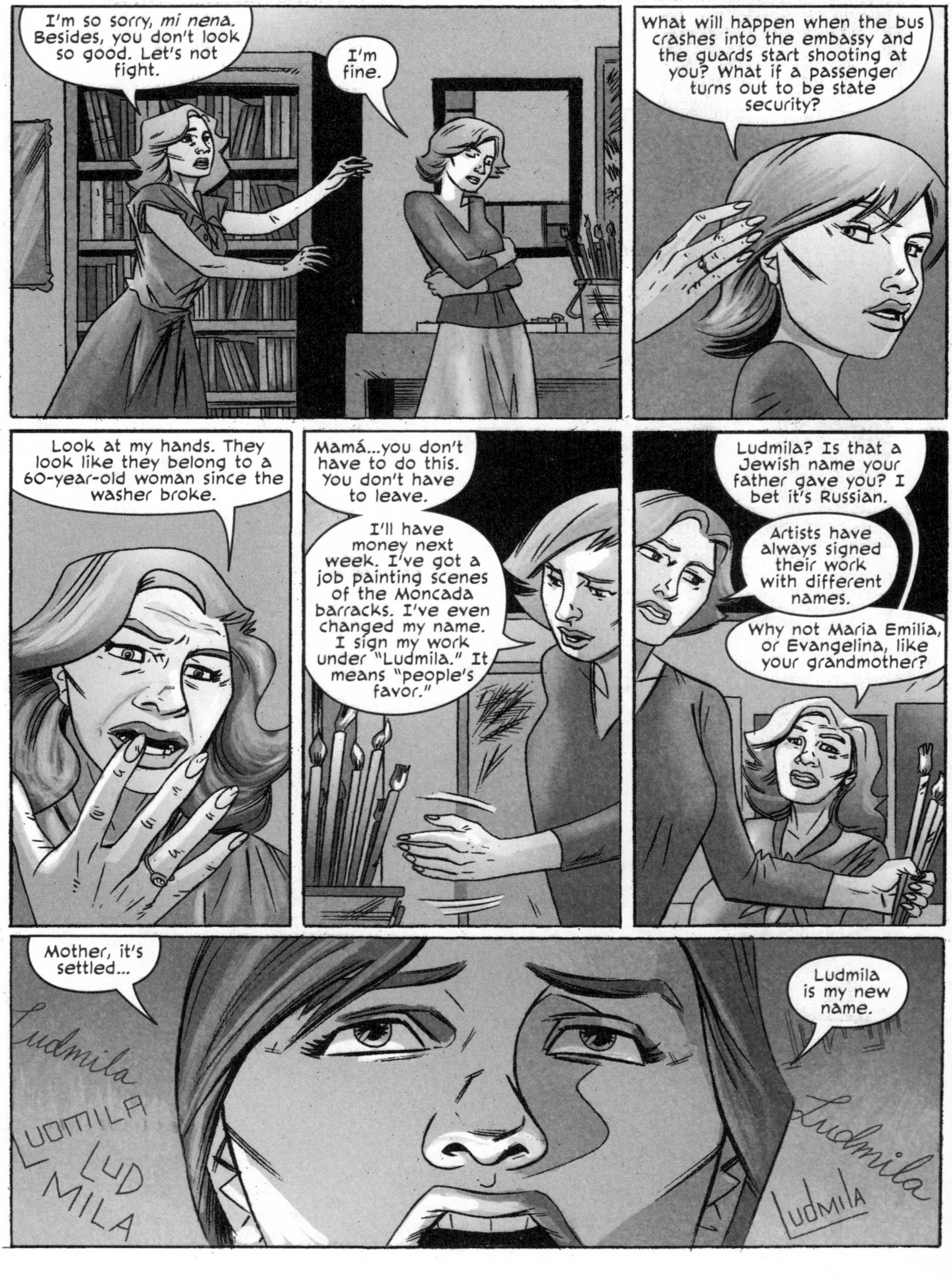
I'm so sorry, *mi nena.* Besides, you don't look so good. Let's not fight.
I'm fine.
What will happen when the bus crashes into the embassy and the guards start shooting at you? What if a passenger turns out to be state security?
Look at my hands. They look like they belong to a 60-year-old woman since the washer broke.
Mamá...you don't have to do this. You don't have to leave.
I'll have money next week. I've got a job painting scenes of the Moncada barracks. I've even changed my name. I sign my work under "Ludmila." It means "people's favor."
Ludmila? Is that a Jewish name your father gave you? I bet it's Russian.
Artists have always signed their work with different names.
Why not Maria Emilia, or Evangelina, like your grandmother?
Mother, it's settled...
Ludmila is my new name.
Ludmila
LUDMILA
LUD
MILA
Ludmila
LUDMILA

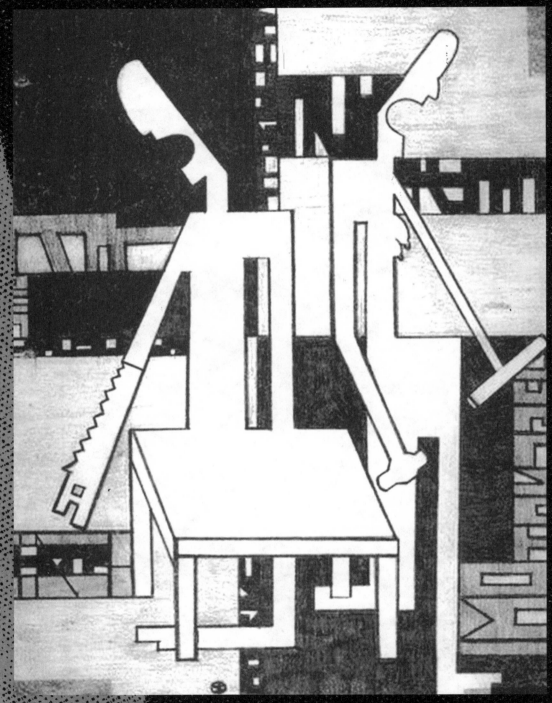

PART THREE

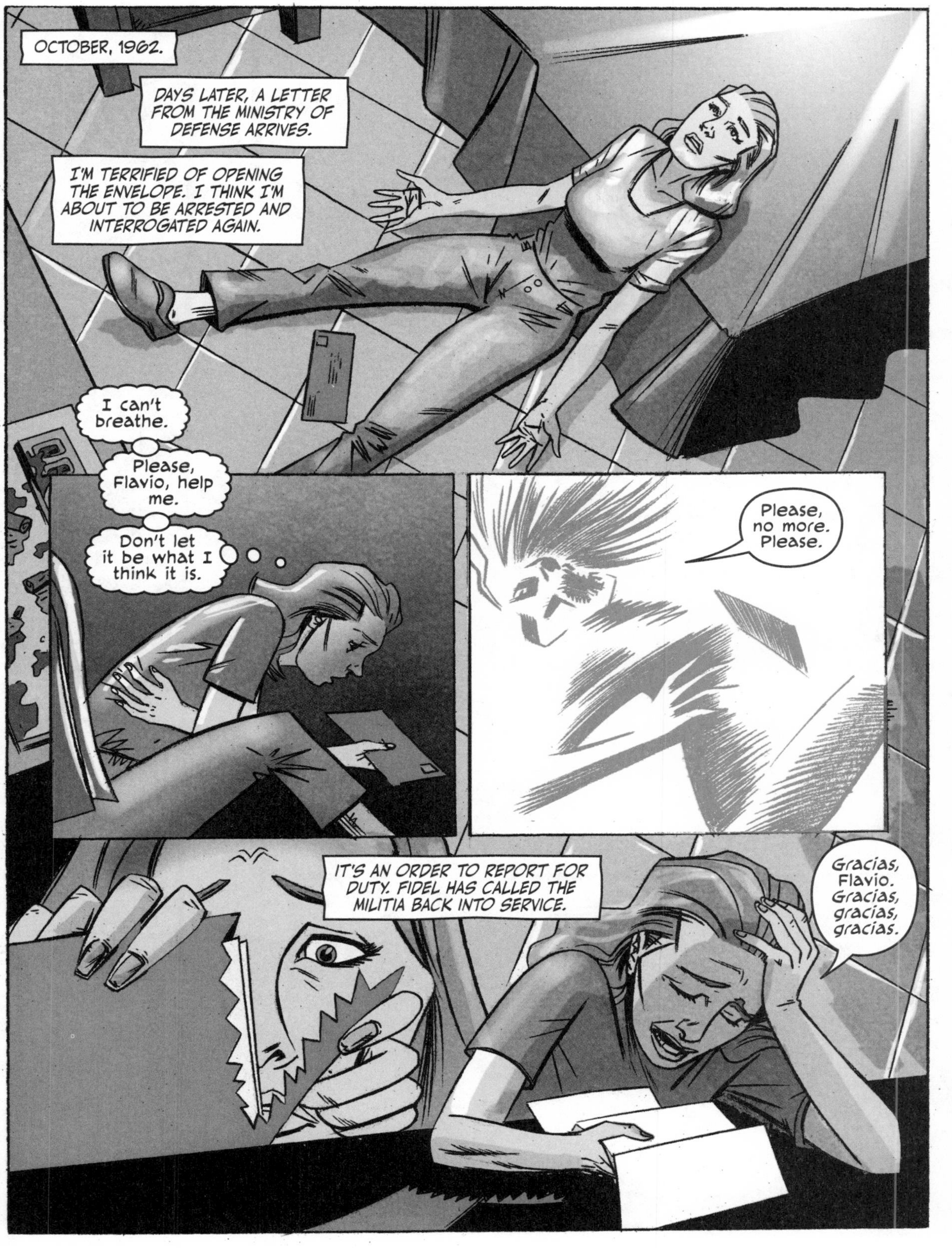

OCTOBER, 1962.
DAYS LATER, A LETTER FROM THE MINISTRY OF DEFENSE ARRIVES.
I'M TERRIFIED OF OPENING THE ENVELOPE. I THINK I'M ABOUT TO BE ARRESTED AND INTERROGATED AGAIN.
I can't breathe.
Please, Flavio, help me.
Don't let it be what I think it is.
Please, no more. Please.
IT'S AN ORDER TO REPORT FOR DUTY. FIDEL HAS CALLED THE MILITIA BACK INTO SERVICE.
Gracias, Flavio. Gracias, gracias, gracias.

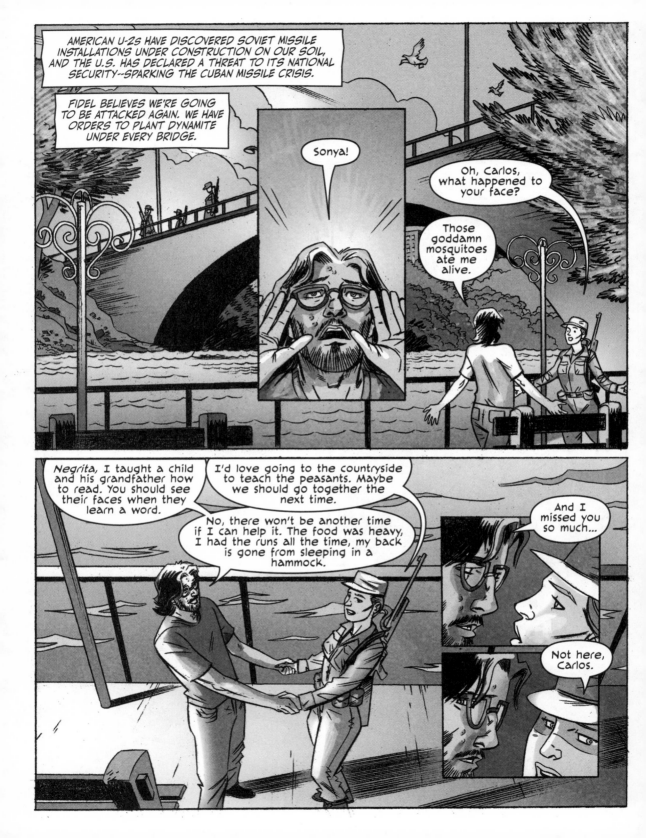

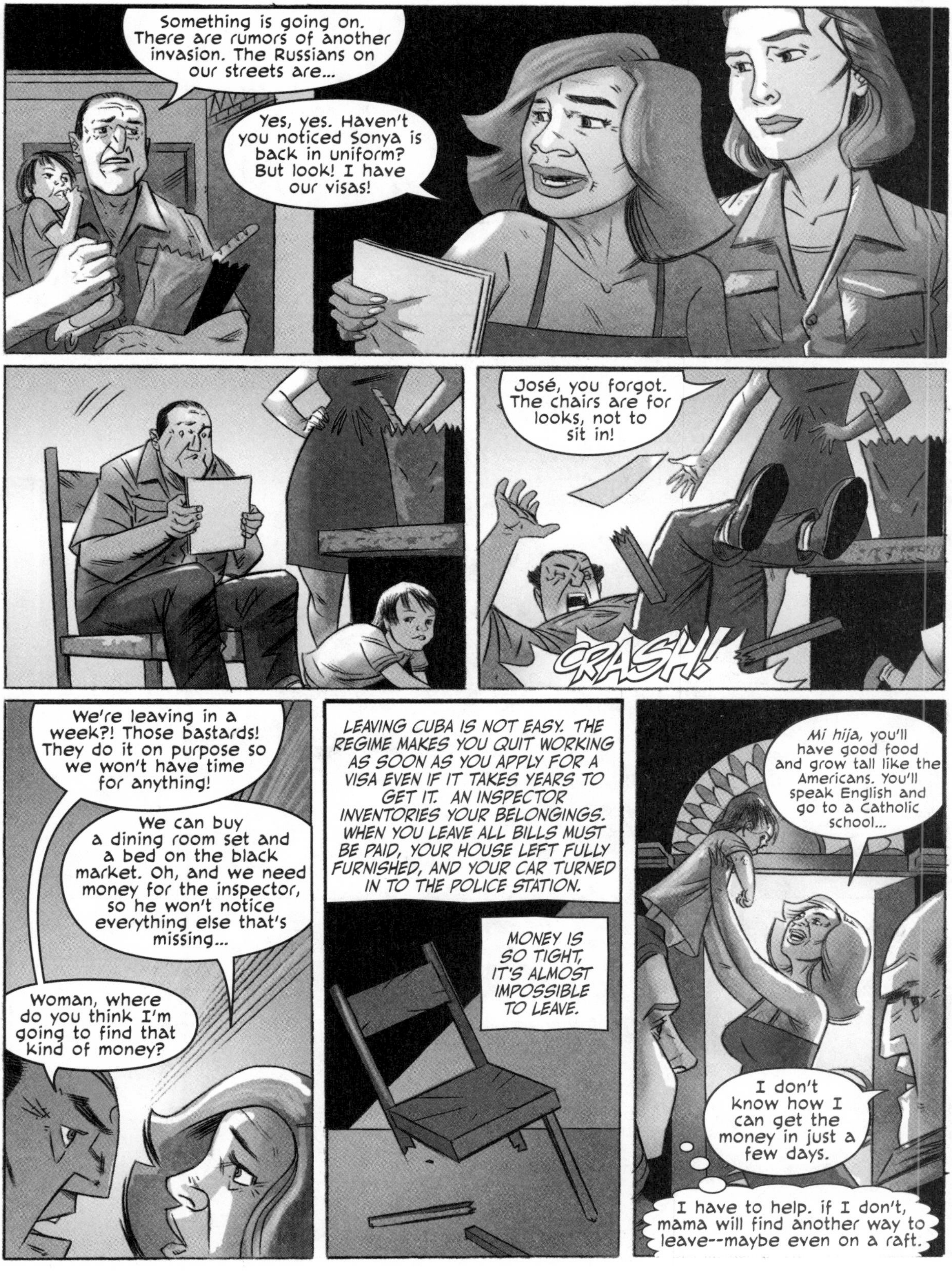

Something is going on. There are rumors of another invasion. The Russians on our streets are...
Yes, yes. Haven't you noticed Sonya is back in uniform? But look! I have our visas!
José, you forgot. The chairs are for looks, not to sit in!
CRASH!
We're leaving in a week?! Those bastards! They do it on purpose so we won't have time for anything!
We can buy a dining room set and a bed on the black market. Oh, and we need money for the inspector, so he won't notice everything else that's missing...
Woman, where do you think I'm going to find that kind of money?
LEAVING CUBA IS NOT EASY. THE REGIME MAKES YOU QUIT WORKING AS SOON AS YOU APPLY FOR A VISA EVEN IF IT TAKES YEARS TO GET IT. AN INSPECTOR INVENTORIES YOUR BELONGINGS. WHEN YOU LEAVE ALL BILLS MUST BE PAID, YOUR HOUSE LEFT FULLY FURNISHED, AND YOUR CAR TURNED IN TO THE POLICE STATION.
MONEY IS SO TIGHT, IT'S ALMOST IMPOSSIBLE TO LEAVE.
Mi hija, you'll have good food and grow tall like the Americans. You'll speak English and go to a Catholic school...
I don't know how I can get the money in just a few days.
I have to help. if I don't, mama will find another way to leave--maybe even on a raft.

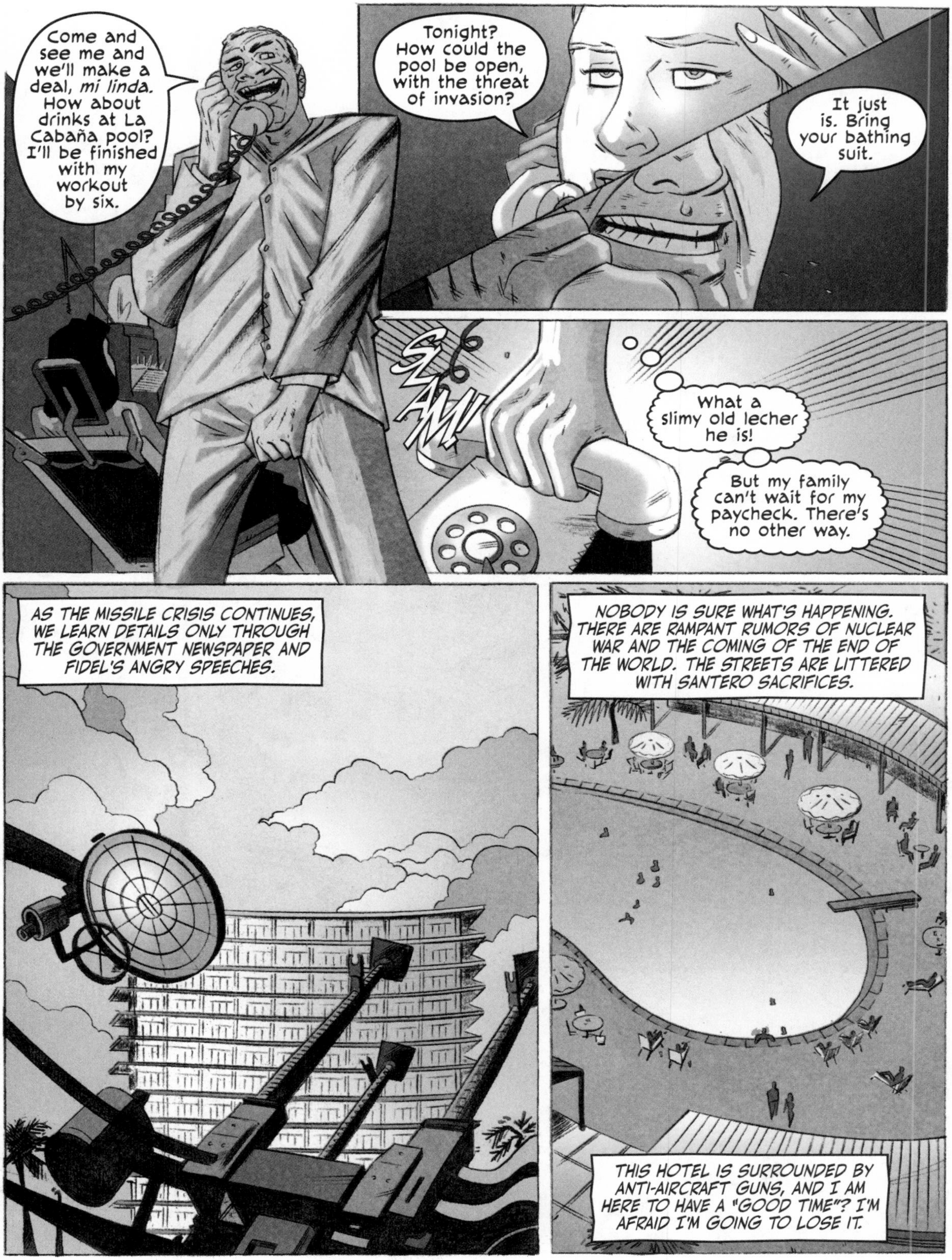
Come and see me and we'll make a deal, *mi linda.* How about drinks at La Cabaña pool? I'll be finished with my workout by six.
Tonight? How could the pool be open, with the threat of invasion?
It just is. Bring your bathing suit.
SLAM!
What a slimy old lecher he is!
But my family can't wait for my paycheck. There's no other way.
AS THE MISSILE CRISIS CONTINUES, WE LEARN DETAILS ONLY THROUGH THE GOVERNMENT NEWSPAPER AND FIDEL'S ANGRY SPEECHES.
NOBODY IS SURE WHAT'S HAPPENING. THERE ARE RAMPANT RUMORS OF NUCLEAR WAR AND THE COMING OF THE END OF THE WORLD. THE STREETS ARE LITTERED WITH SANTERO SACRIFICES.
THIS HOTEL IS SURROUNDED BY ANTI-AIRCRAFT GUNS, AND I AM HERE TO HAVE A "GOOD TIME"? I'M AFRAID I'M GOING TO LOSE IT.

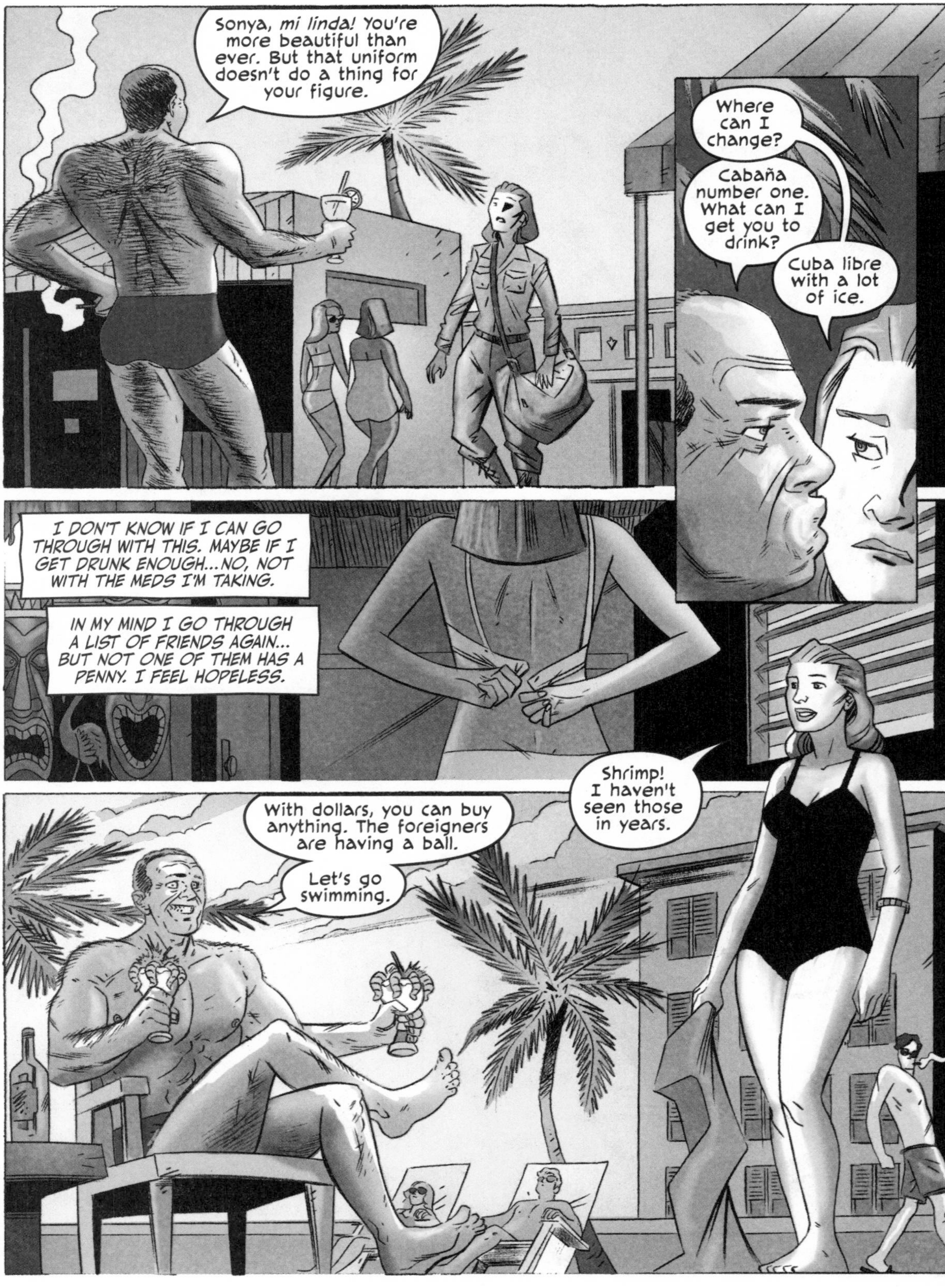
Sonya, *mi linda!* You're more beautiful than ever. But that uniform doesn't do a thing for your figure.
Where can I change?
Cabaña number one. What can I get you to drink?
Cuba libre with a lot of ice.
I DON'T KNOW IF I CAN GO THROUGH WITH THIS. MAYBE IF I GET DRUNK ENOUGH...NO, NOT WITH THE MEDS I'M TAKING.
IN MY MIND I GO THROUGH A LIST OF FRIENDS AGAIN... BUT NOT ONE OF THEM HAS A PENNY. I FEEL HOPELESS.
Shrimp! I haven't seen those in years.
With dollars, you can buy anything. The foreigners are having a ball.
Let's go swimming.

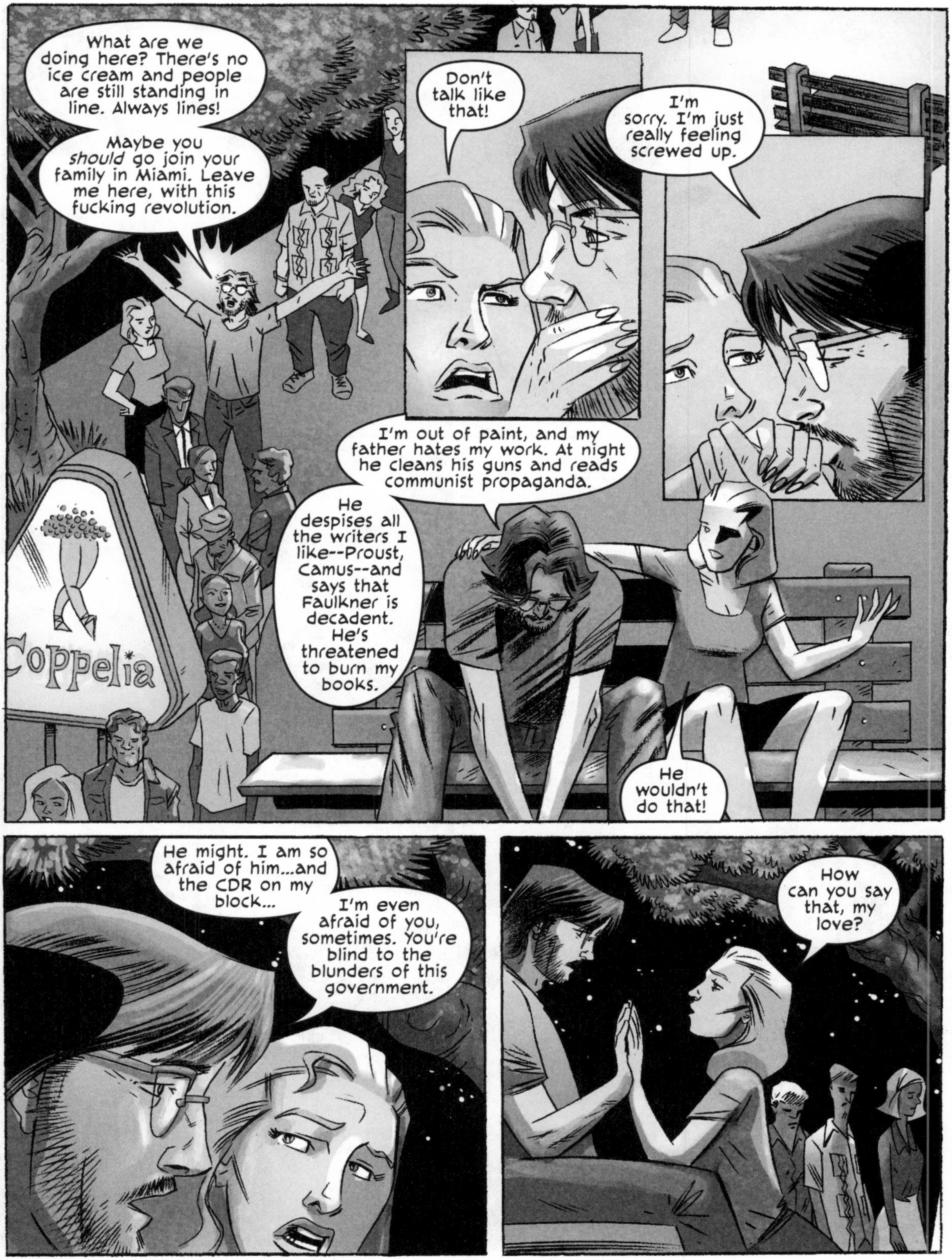
What are we doing here? There's no ice cream and people are still standing in line. Always lines!
Maybe you *should* go join your family in Miami. Leave me here, with this fucking revolution.
Don't talk like that!
I'm sorry. I'm just really feeling screwed up.
I'm out of paint, and my father hates my work. At night he cleans his guns and reads communist propaganda.
He despises all the writers I like--Proust, Camus--and says that Faulkner is decadent. He's threatened to burn my books.
Coppelia
He wouldn't do that!
He might. I am so afraid of him...and the CDR on my block...
I'm even afraid of you, sometimes. You're blind to the blunders of this government.
How can you say that, my love?

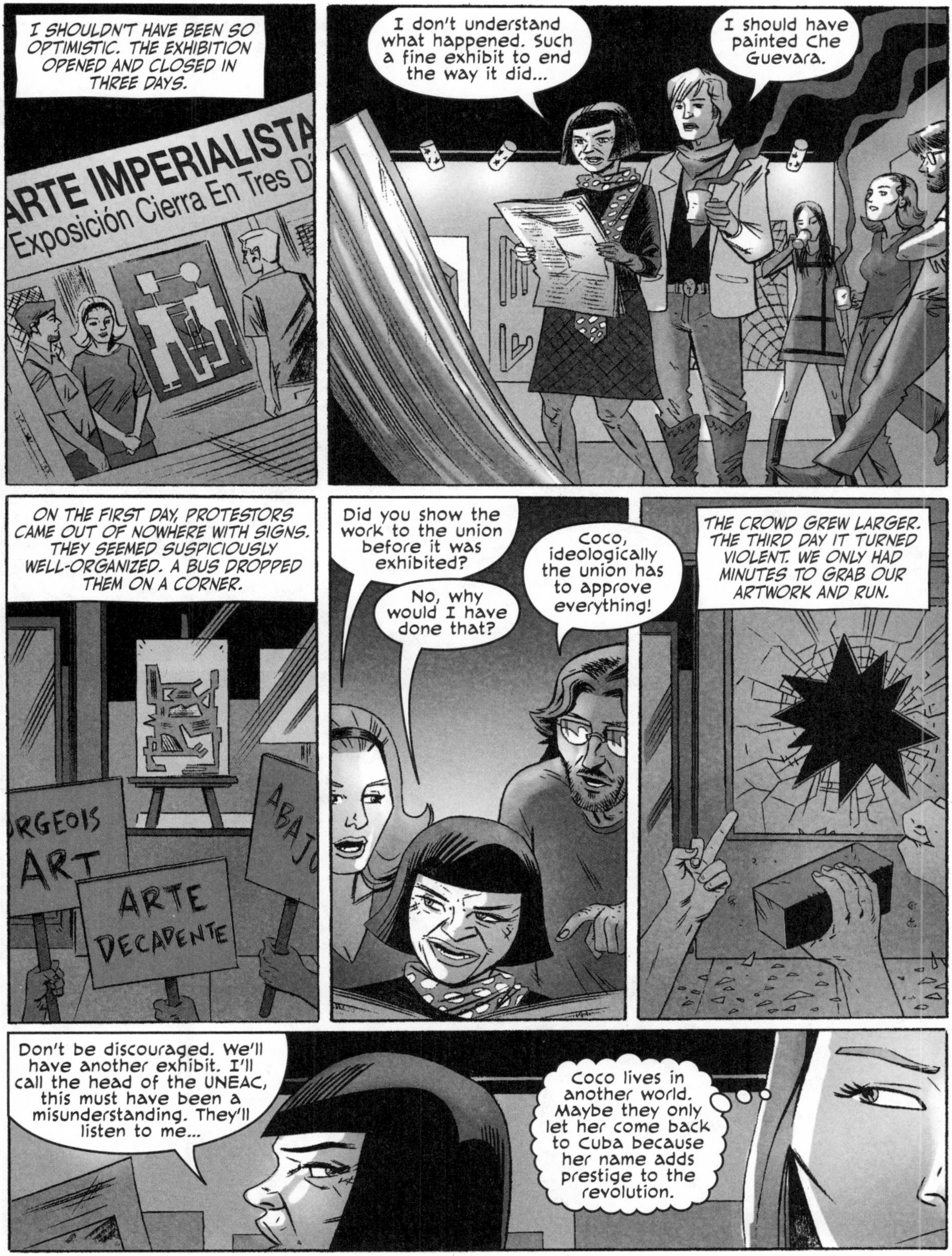
I SHOULDN'T HAVE BEEN SO OPTIMISTIC. THE EXHIBITION OPENED AND CLOSED IN THREE DAYS.
ARTE IMPERIALISTA
Exposición Cierra En Tres D
I don't understand what happened. Such a fine exhibit to end the way it did...
I should have painted Che Guevara.
ON THE FIRST DAY, PROTESTORS CAME OUT OF NOWHERE WITH SIGNS. THEY SEEMED SUSPICIOUSLY WELL-ORGANIZED. A BUS DROPPED THEM ON A CORNER.
RGEOIS ART
ARTE DECADENTE
ABAJO
Did you show the work to the union before it was exhibited?
No, why would I have done that?
Coco, ideologically the union has to approve everything!
THE CROWD GREW LARGER. THE THIRD DAY IT TURNED VIOLENT. WE ONLY HAD MINUTES TO GRAB OUR ARTWORK AND RUN.
Don't be discouraged. We'll have another exhibit. I'll call the head of the UNEAC, this must have been a misunderstanding. They'll listen to me...
Coco lives in another world. Maybe they only let her come back to Cuba because her name adds prestige to the revolution.

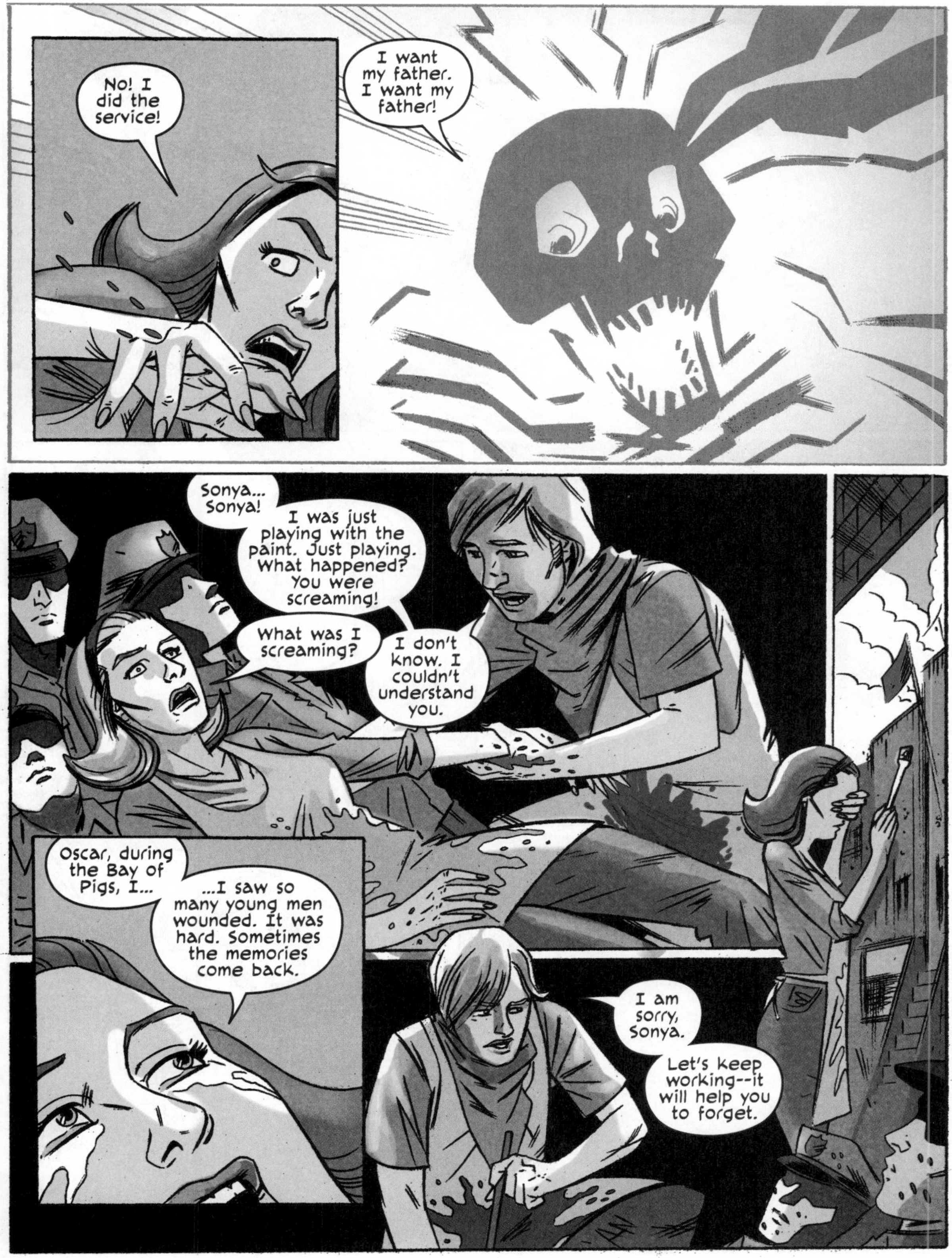
No! I did the service!
I want my father. I want my father!
Sonya... Sonya!
I was just playing with the paint. Just playing. What happened? You were screaming!
What was I screaming?
I don't know. I couldn't understand you.
Oscar, during the Bay of Pigs, I...
...I saw so many young men wounded. It was hard. Sometimes the memories come back.
I am sorry, Sonya.
Let's keep working--it will help you to forget.

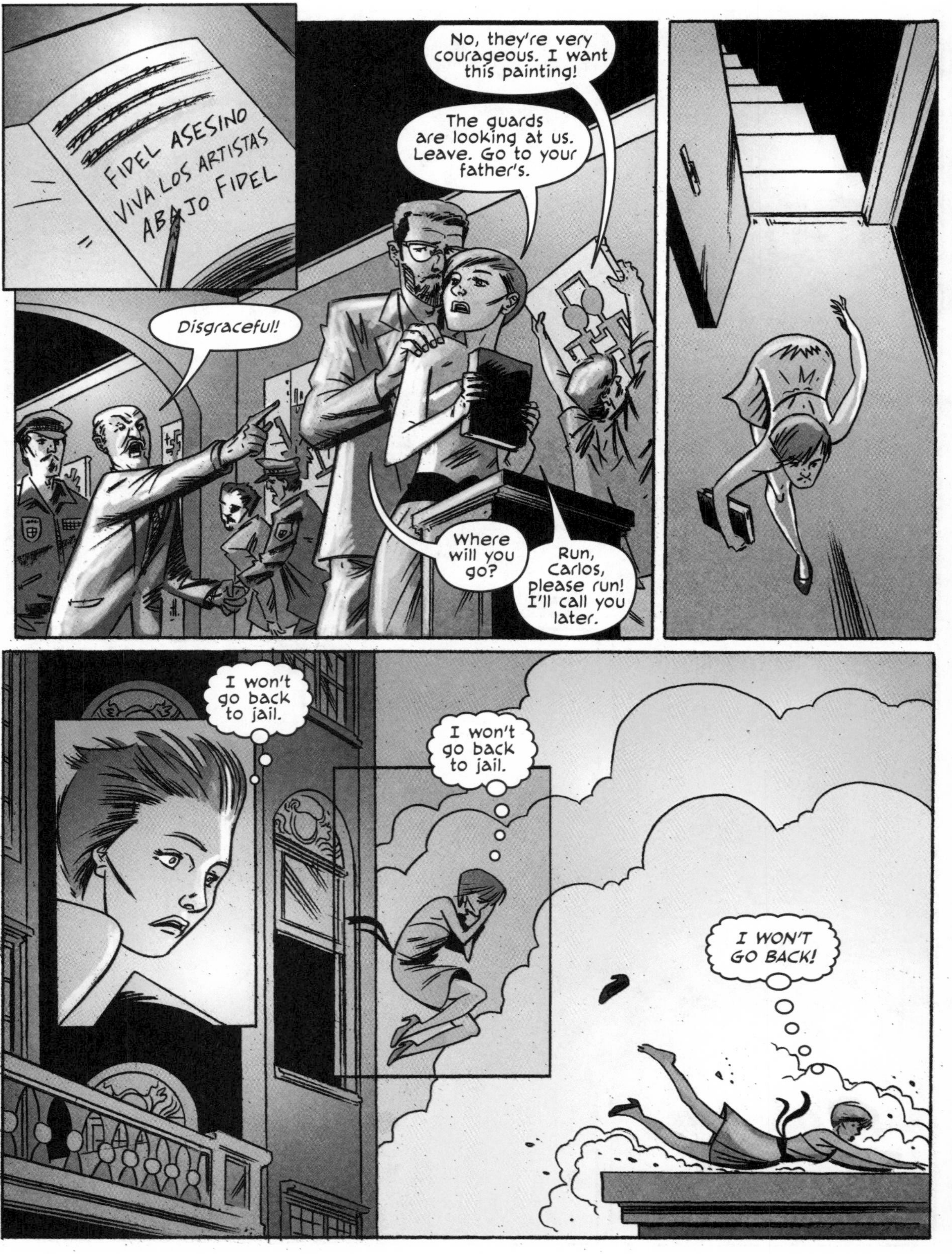
FIDEL ASESINO
VIVA LOS ARTISTAS
ABAJO FIDEL
The guards are looking at us. Leave. Go to your father's.
No, they're very courageous. I want this painting!
Disgraceful!
Where will you go?
Run, Carlos, please run! I'll call you later.
I won't go back to jail.
I won't go back to jail.
I WON'T GO BACK!

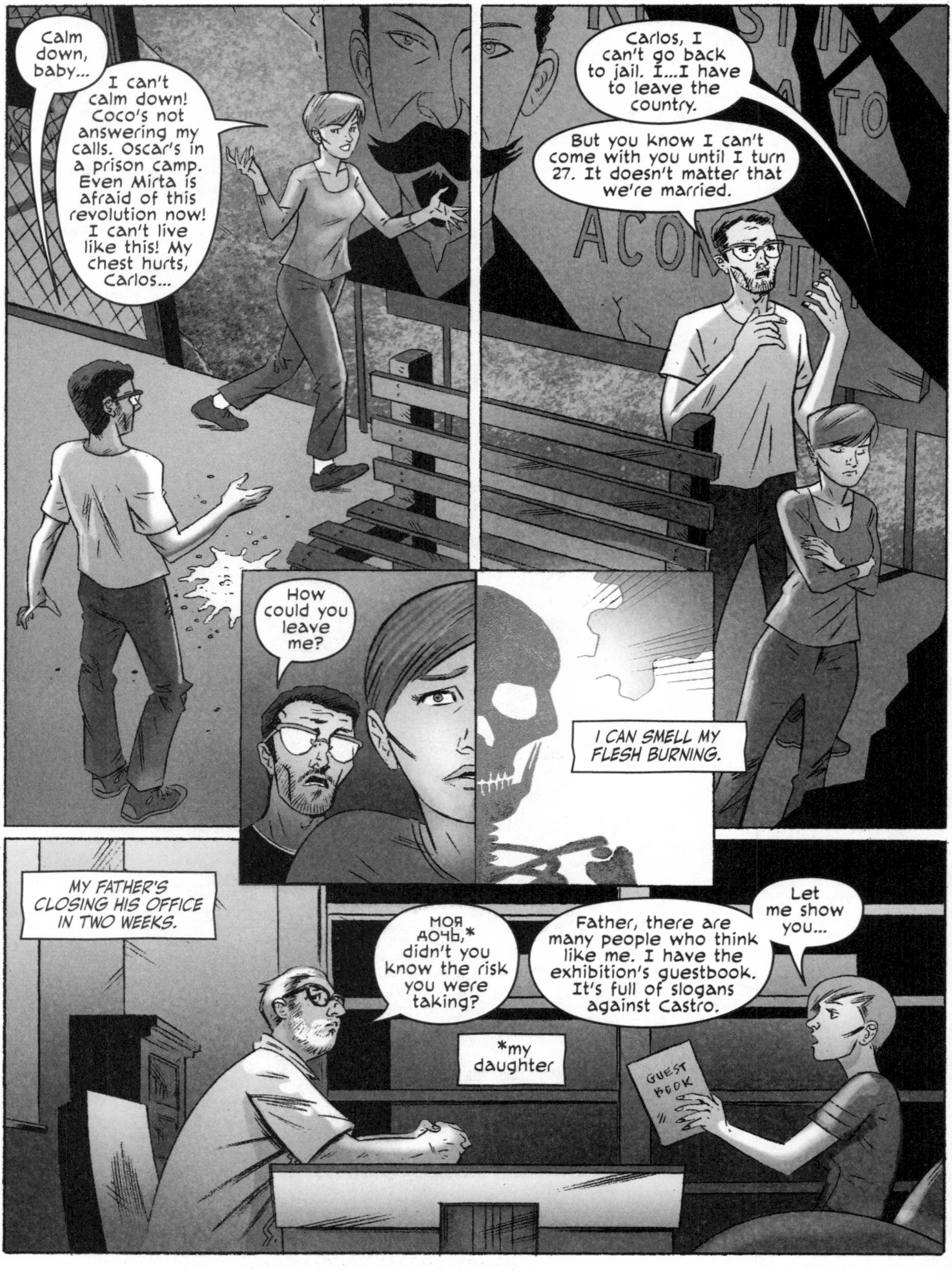
Calm down, baby...
I can't calm down! Coco's not answering my calls. Oscar's in a prison camp. Even Mirta is afraid of this revolution now! I can't live like this! My chest hurts, Carlos...
Carlos, I can't go back to jail. I...I have to leave the country.
But you know I can't come with you until I turn 27. It doesn't matter that we're married.
How could you leave me?
I CAN SMELL MY FLESH BURNING.
MY FATHER'S CLOSING HIS OFFICE IN TWO WEEKS.
моя дочь,* didn't you know the risk you were taking?
Father, there are many people who think like me. I have the exhibition's guestbook. It's full of slogans against Castro.
Let me show you...
*my daughter
GUEST BOOK

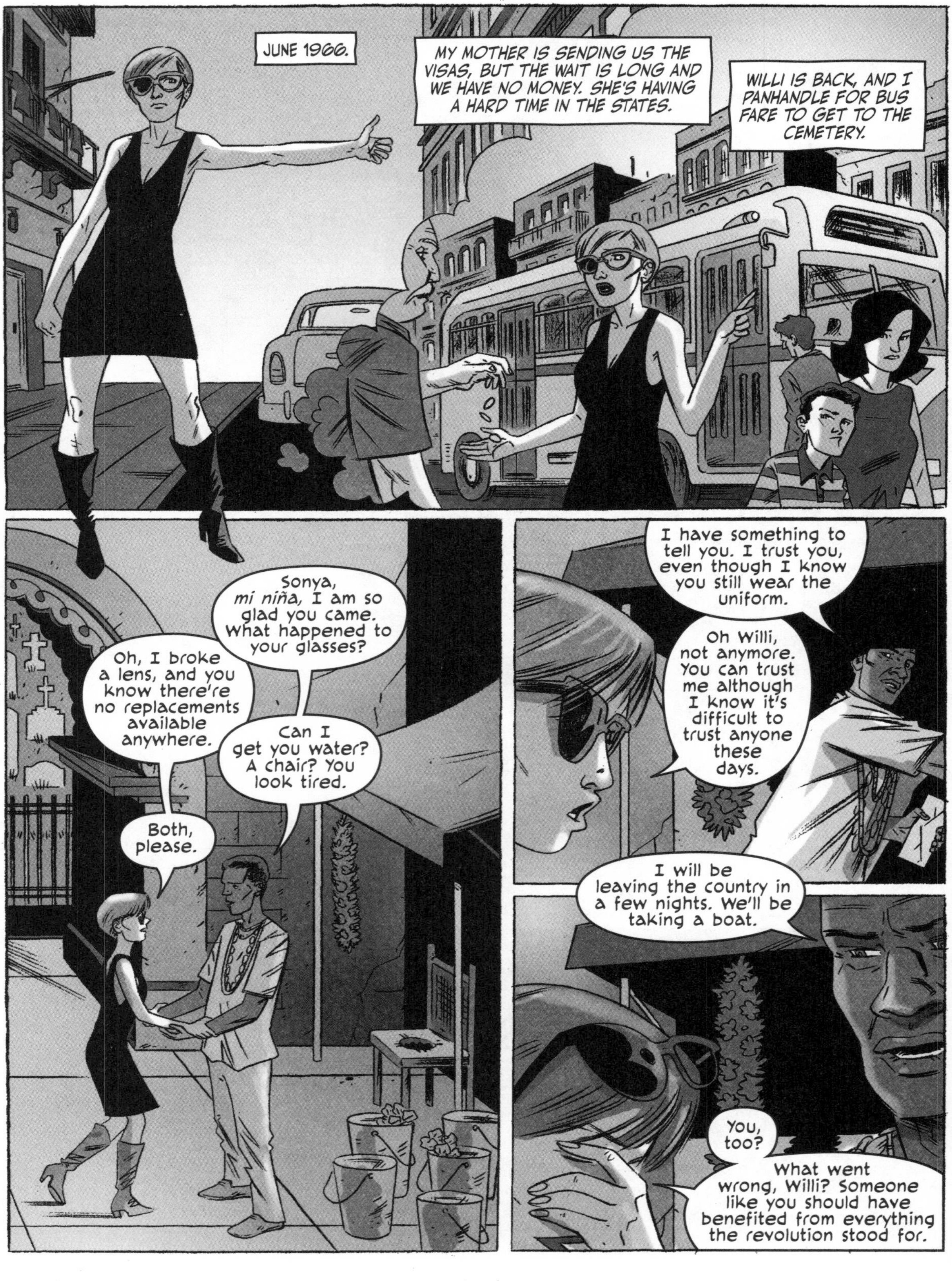
JUNE 1966.
MY MOTHER IS SENDING US THE VISAS, BUT THE WAIT IS LONG AND WE HAVE NO MONEY. SHE'S HAVING A HARD TIME IN THE STATES.
WILLI IS BACK, AND I PANHANDLE FOR BUS FARE TO GET TO THE CEMETERY.
Sonya, *mi niña,* I am so glad you came. What happened to your glasses?
Oh, I broke a lens, and you know there're no replacements available anywhere.
Can I get you water? A chair? You look tired.
Both, please.
I have something to tell you. I trust you, even though I know you still wear the uniform.
Oh Willi, not anymore. You can trust me although I know it's difficult to trust anyone these days.
I will be leaving the country in a few nights. We'll be taking a boat.
You, too?
What went wrong, Willi? Someone like you should have benefited from everything the revolution stood for.

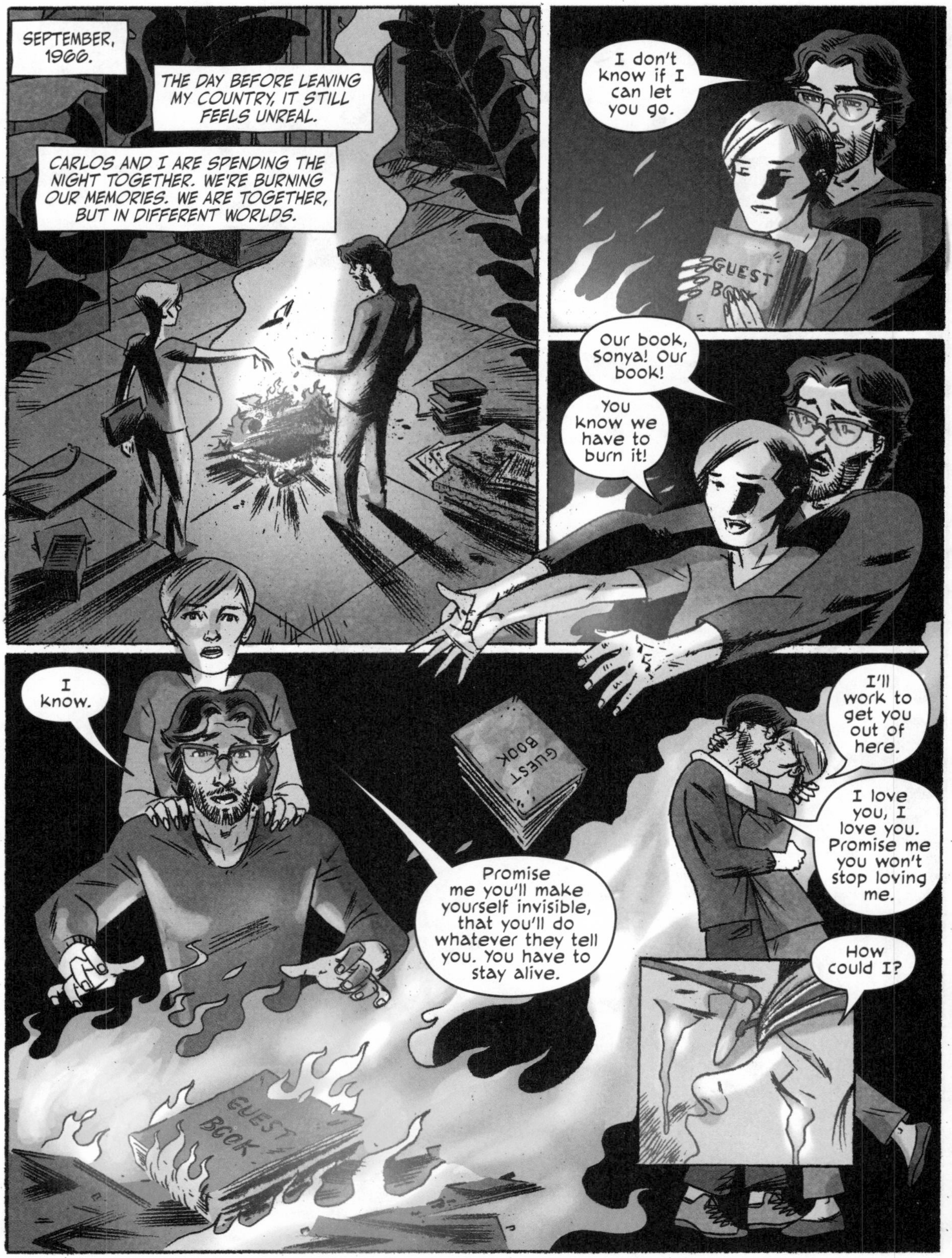
SEPTEMBER, 1966.
THE DAY BEFORE LEAVING MY COUNTRY, IT STILL FEELS UNREAL.
CARLOS AND I ARE SPENDING THE NIGHT TOGETHER. WE'RE BURNING OUR MEMORIES. WE ARE TOGETHER, BUT IN DIFFERENT WORLDS.
I don't know if I can let you go.
GUEST BOOK
Our book, Sonya! Our book!
You know we have to burn it!
I know.
GUEST BOOK
Promise me you'll make yourself invisible, that you'll do whatever they tell you. You have to stay alive.
GUEST BOOK
I'll work to get you out of here.
I love you, I love you. Promise me you won't stop loving me.
How could I?

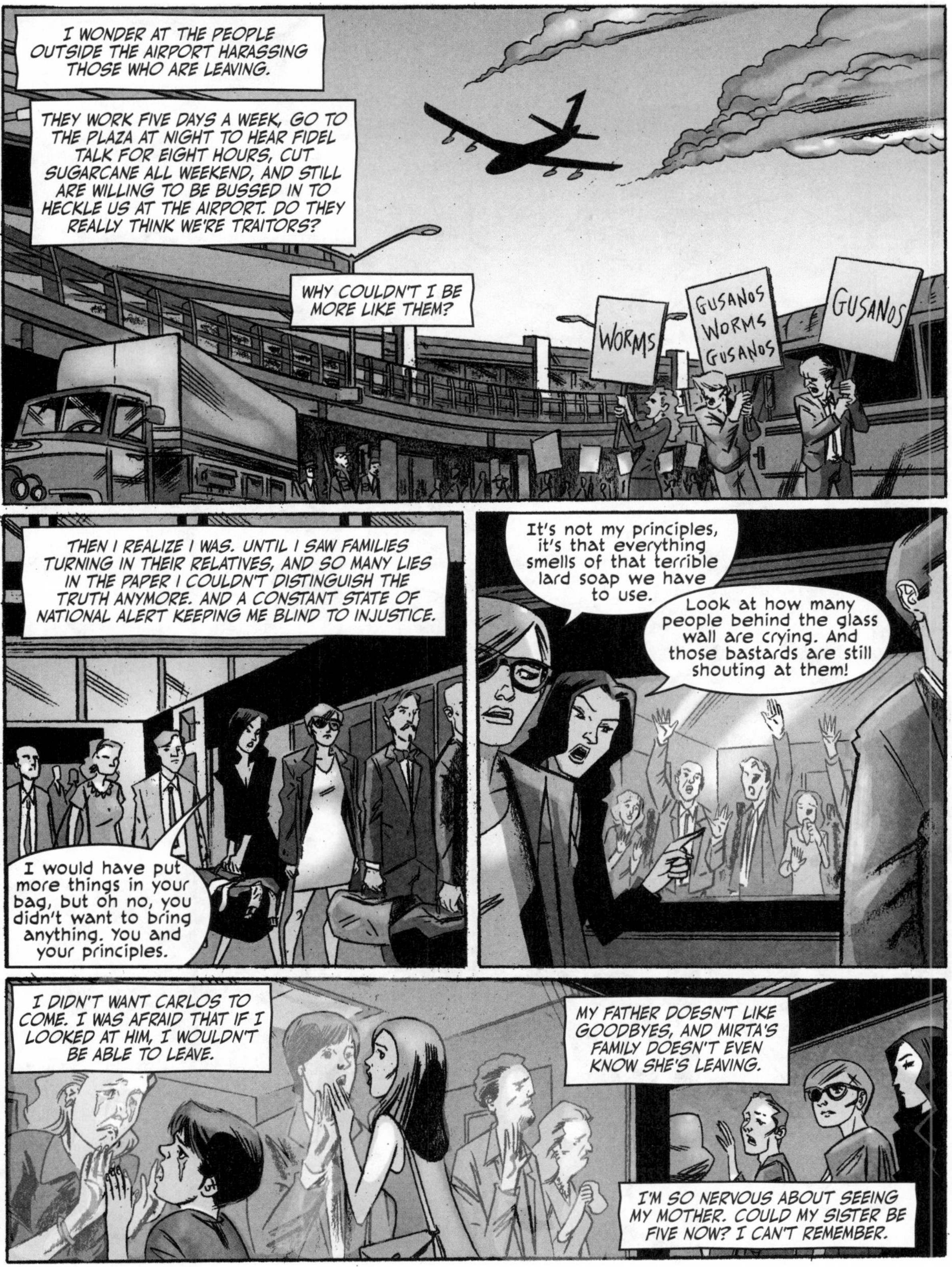

I WONDER AT THE PEOPLE OUTSIDE THE AIRPORT HARASSING THOSE WHO ARE LEAVING.
THEY WORK FIVE DAYS A WEEK, GO TO THE PLAZA AT NIGHT TO HEAR FIDEL TALK FOR EIGHT HOURS, CUT SUGARCANE ALL WEEKEND, AND STILL ARE WILLING TO BE BUSSED IN TO HECKLE US AT THE AIRPORT. DO THEY REALLY THINK WE'RE TRAITORS?
WHY COULDN'T I BE MORE LIKE THEM?
WORMS
GUSANOS WORMS GUSANOS
GUSANOS
THEN I REALIZE I WAS. UNTIL I SAW FAMILIES TURNING IN THEIR RELATIVES, AND SO MANY LIES IN THE PAPER I COULDN'T DISTINGUISH THE TRUTH ANYMORE. AND A CONSTANT STATE OF NATIONAL ALERT KEEPING ME BLIND TO INJUSTICE.
I would have put more things in your bag, but oh no, you didn't want to bring anything. You and your principles.
It's not my principles, it's that everything smells of that terrible lard soap we have to use.
Look at how many people behind the glass wall are crying. And those bastards are still shouting at them!
I DIDN'T WANT CARLOS TO COME. I WAS AFRAID THAT IF I LOOKED AT HIM, I WOULDN'T BE ABLE TO LEAVE.
MY FATHER DOESN'T LIKE GOODBYES, AND MIRTA'S FAMILY DOESN'T EVEN KNOW SHE'S LEAVING.
I'M SO NERVOUS ABOUT SEEING MY MOTHER. COULD MY SISTER BE FIVE NOW? I CAN'T REMEMBER.

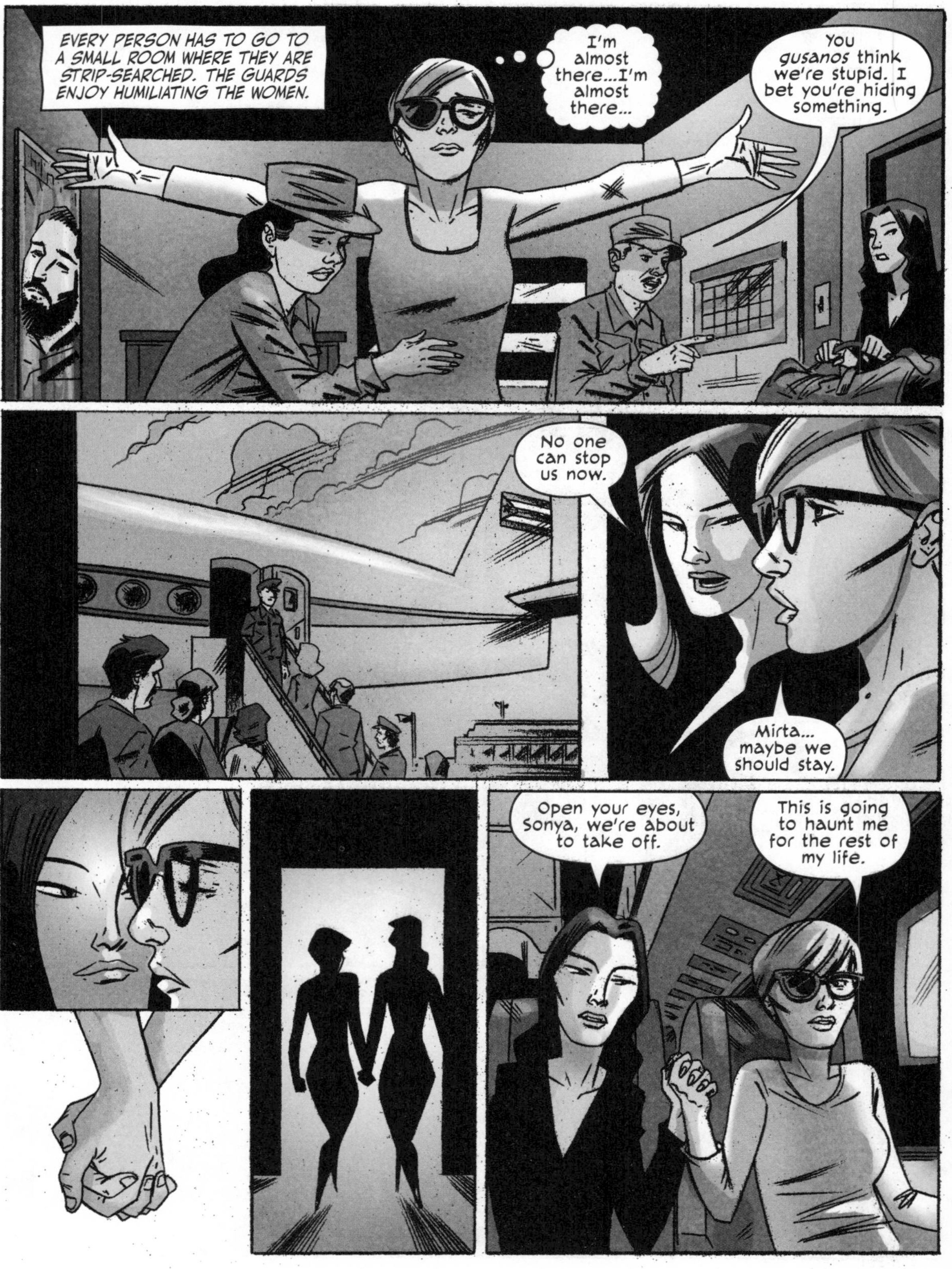
EVERY PERSON HAS TO GO TO A SMALL ROOM WHERE THEY ARE STRIP-SEARCHED. THE GUARDS ENJOY HUMILIATING THE WOMEN.
I'm almost there...I'm almost there...
You gusanos think we're stupid. I bet you're hiding something.
No one can stop us now.
Mirta... maybe we should stay.
Open your eyes, Sonya, we're about to take off.
This is going to haunt me for the rest of my life.

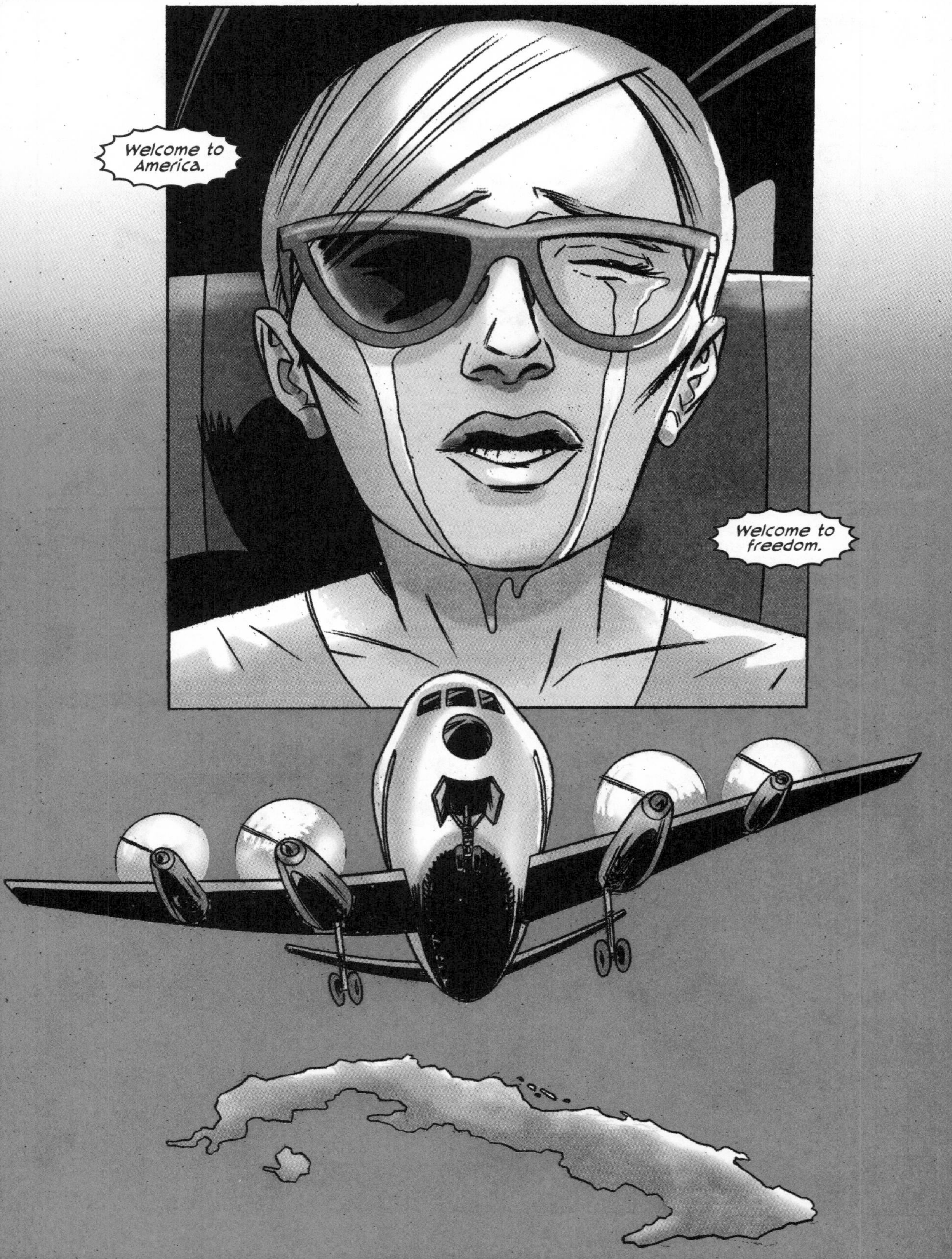
Welcome to America.
Welcome to freedom.